Asperger Syndrome and Employment

Adults Speak Out about Asperger Syndrome

Edited by Genevieve Edmonds and Luke Beardon

Jessica Kingsley Publishers
London and Philadelphia

First published in 2008
by Jessica Kingsley Publishers
116 Pentonville Road
London N1 9JB, UK
and
400 Market Street, Suite 400
Philadelphia, PA 19106, USA

www.jkp.com

Copyright © Jessica Kingsley Publishers 2008

Library of Congress Cataloging in Publication Data
A CIP catalog record for this book is available from the Library of Congress

British Library Cataloguing in Publication Data
A CIP catalogue record for this book is available from the British Library

ISBN 978 1 84310 648 7

Printed and bound in Great Britain by
Athenaeum Press, Gateshead, Tyne and Wear

AUTHOR

TITLE   Asperger Syndrome & Employment

Please return/renew this item by the last date shown
Thank you for using your college library

SHEFFIELD COLLEGE - CASTLE CENTRE
Tel. 0114 260 2134

Contents

Acknowledgements

To all the authors contributing to the series – many thanks for your time and effort in helping to produce these books.

Dedication

To all those individuals with AS who have shared their lives with us; we are forever indebted to you all. (Genevieve Edmonds and Luke Beardon)

Preface to the Series

Genevieve Edmonds

As an adult with Asperger Syndrome (AS) and as someone who works within the field of autism as a trainer and consultant, I am all too aware of the situation facing adults with AS at present. For many (the majority, in reality), it is not good: it is characterized by a lack of understanding, support, respect and appropriate services. The aim of this book series is to make available the experiences of adults with AS on pertinent life issues, so that services and individuals may be able to learn what to do to set up and improve support systems for them.

More people are being diagnosed with autism spectrum disorder (ASD) now than ever before, though the question remains unanswered whether this is as a result of an 'autism epidemic' or as a result of better diagnostic expertise. We do know that autism is a lifelong condition (it doesn't end at the age of 18) with no known cure. Although some tried and tested models of support do exist, there are few which address the needs of adults with AS. Much of the research available around autism appears to be centred around the origins of autism rather than looking at the reality of living with it.

Existing services appear to be guided predominantly by the well-known 'Triad of Impairments' model of autism (Wing and Gould 1979), which outlines the three areas of difficulty (though we should be looking at *difference*). It leaves adults with AS at the centre of a model that generates deficit-based, rather than person-centred, thinking and approaches. This purely medicalized view of AS is in fact at odds with the intentions of the Government in the UK. In 2006, a note was written to clarify the current picture for individuals with ASDs in transition and adulthood, 'Better Services for People with Autistic Spectrum Disorders (ASD)' (Department of Health 2006). It encourages social care organizations to develop local agendas for service improvement for adults with ASD.

What is needed is a move away from a medicalized view of autism and AS: individuals with AS should be understood as people who process the social world 'differently' rather than in a 'disordered' fashion, and support should centre around the understanding that the *disability* element of AS is born from individuals' lack of *opportunity* to process information differently, and in a way that makes sense to them. Our hope is that with the help of this series better support can begin to emerge for adults with AS so that they can begin to live more fulfilled and happier lives, which sadly too few do at this time.

Bibliography

Department of Health (2006) 'Better Services for People with Autistic Spectrum Disorders (ASD).' Available at www.dh.gov.uk/en/Publicationsandstatistics/ Publications/PublicationsPolicyAndGuidance/DH_065242. Accessed 2 October 2007.

Wing, L. and Gould, J. (1979) 'Severe impairments of social interaction and associated abnormalities in children: Epidemiology and classification.' *Journal of Autism and Childhood Schizophrenia*, 9, 11–29.

Introduction

Luke Beardon

On paper, is there anything at all that suggests a person with AS would not make a good employee? Well, that depends on the person and the job. But, being highly general about it, one could put forward the argument that the answer is a resounding 'No', that there is no reason at all why an individual with AS would make any worse an employee than their neurotypical (NT) counterparts. Indeed, it could also be argued that many of the so-called characteristics of AS – those neurological and developmental differences that define individuals with AS – are conducive to making an excellent employee.

Some characteristics include:

- differences in communication
- social understanding
- Theory of Mind
- executive functioning
- sensory processing.

Communication

All too often we have a tendency to look at a negative side of AS, without truly appreciating the skills and positives that AS provide. For example, we note that individuals with AS may misinterpret what is being said to them and thus cause problems at work. However, I would suggest that in the majority of cases, the individual is not misinterpreting what is being said, but is, if there is such a thing, being too accurate in their interpretation. The key lies with the word 'interpret' – if NTs were accurate, direct and honest in their instruction then there would not be any need for interpretation. If employers, line managers, co-workers recognized that just as much fault lay at their door because of the lack of clarity in their own verbal communication, and were to respond accordingly, then problems would be minimized. As a general rule, written forms of communication are far better than verbal. Written communication tends to lack as many ambiguities, and it has the advantage of being a visual reminder for those who may have delays in their processing of verbal communication. In this day and age, with email becoming widespread, there is even less need to impart instruction in a face-to-face verbal style. If someone has a tendency to take language literally (i.e. accurately) surely this is an asset? I have been a line manager myself (to NT staff) and I would have loved the opportunity to provide them with clear direct instruction that I knew would be taken exactly as it was intended! Communication need not be a problem, and can be turned into a positive as long as employees manage their own fallibility for saying the wrong thing.

Social understanding

It is true that the workplace is often one in which friendships and relationships develop. However, I have yet to meet anyone who puts on their application form, or states at interview, that the social opportunities within a post are what drove them to apply. Similarly, if I was interviewing for a post and a candidate told me they were applying for the job to socialize and make friends I would instantly be on my guard. Why, then, it social interaction deemed so important in the workplace? How can it be that it often transcends the real reason for being there – i.e. to actually do a job? The answer, of course, is because NTs are, by nature, generally social beings, and social interaction is an important part of daily life. This should not preclude an individual with AS, however. With clear rules and boundaries around social expectation within the workplace, as well as an understanding from those within the workplace, there is no reason why a difference in social understanding need be a problem for doing a job, and doing it well – unless, of course, part of the job itself includes elements of social interaction. Even then, there are plenty of individuals with AS who make remarkably good employees in what may, theoretically, seem improbable posts – customer services, support work and so on. The diversity of the population is such that there is no line of work that can be discounted as unsuitable for an individual with AS.

Theory of Mind

What springs to mind most when it comes to a working environment and Theory of Mind, are the number of individuals with AS that I know who *use* their AS Theory of Mind to support others who have similar thinking styles. So many individuals who are told they lack a Theory of Mind demonstrate quite the opposite when it comes to other people with AS. I know of several individuals who have devoted their time – almost always unpaid – to support other people with AS, and such individuals often do a far better job of it than NT support mechanisms. When it comes to other working environments, where are the person specifications that state an employee must have the ability to mind read in order to do their job properly? I've yet to see any. By implication, then, why would a different Theory of Mind affect an individual's ability to work? In reality, many of the problems associated with this are not, in fact, performance-related, but may well be interpersonal-related. Saying the 'wrong' thing at the 'wrong' time, for example, can lead to problems if others are not aware as to why this may have occurred. Being seen as overly blunt or to the point may have a similar effect. Once again, however, this suggests that the problem lies just as much with the rest of the workforce – if there was a greater understanding then such directness can be turned from a negative to a positive. How many times, sitting in a meeting, have I really wanted to say something but have not done so for fear of being too direct or challenging? And yet it is exactly by being direct and challenging (in the 'right' way) that we can instigate effective change and progression. Seeing it and telling it 'how it really is' can be a huge benefit to organizations and business – cue someone with AS!

Executive functioning

Some individuals with AS may find it difficult to organize time, prioritize or manage workloads. Personally, I am also rubbish at all of the above. This does not mean that an individual is incapable of working effectively –

simply that they may require different tools to support them in the most appropriate way. Knowing exactly what is expected, by a specific time, in a specific order is a great help to many individuals, and does not take any great adjustments in work to achieve. Many individuals, on the other hand, are extremely ordered and precise as a result of their executive functioning skills. Such individuals may be excellent at organizing and keeping order in what may otherwise be a chaotic environment – yet another example of skills related to AS, rather than problems arising because of it.

Sensory processing

To have the opportunity to work in an environment that suits an individual's sensory needs is as important to some people as a ramp allowing access is for a person in a wheelchair. For many individuals it is a necessity, not a preference. To be forced into working in an unsuitable environment is not only discriminatory but hazardous to a person's mental well-being and emotional stability. It is incredibly difficult for many NTs to have any understanding of the sensory needs of an individual, and almost as difficult to have any degree of acceptance. Partly it is the 'invisible' nature of sensory issues; partly it is because many NTs are too non-empathic to understand that other people will process the environment in a greatly differing way to themselves. A wheelchair is concrete, obvious – with clear repercussions in the work environment. Sensory issues for the person with AS are not like that – they are not as obvious, not as clear-cut – but for some, they are far more far-reaching in terms of impact. Providing the individual with suitable sensory environment in which to work would greatly reduce a number of the problems faced by them, and allow the individual to fulfil their potential – often with results that surprise many employees.

Reasonable adjustments

It is now law that reasonable adjustments must be made by employees to ensure that individuals with AS are not discriminated against. Unfortunately, what constitutes a reasonable adjustment is fairly open to question. As so many people have a poor understanding of AS – or, perhaps worse, think they have a good understanding simply because they have known one other person – it is likely that it will take time and effort to provide the right environment in which to work. Another problem, which can be a major one, is that some changes will not be around pragmatic environmental issues, but around the behaviour of NTs themselves. For some reason this seems to be one of the most difficult things to change, despite the fact that it can become very clear that it is the NT behaviour that is causing the discrimination as much as anything else. Some of the ways in which NT behaviour can change that may be useful include:

- Change the way in which communication takes place. Do not, for example, assume that verbal communication is always the most effective way of exchanging information or giving instruction.

- Socially interact in a way suited to the individual; for example, some people will see work as work, not a time for social exchanges that may have little or no relevance to them. In such circumstances avoid social exchanges altogether.

- Ensure that social boundaries are clear and adhered to. For example, if work colleagues see themselves as colleagues and not potential friends, then do not give the wrong impression to the individual with AS. If being honest to the point of being blunt is a problem for NTs, imagine how confusing life is for someone with AS who may expect the same kind of honesty. Thus, in answer to the question, 'Are you my friend?', ensure that honest replies are forthcoming, as opposed to the more usual NT response of trying to be tactful – and not entirely honest. This can be confusing and misleading.

- Never judge the person with AS or make them feel that they need to socially interact if they do not wish to do so.

- Make sure that any instructions are clear to the point of no ambiguity. In addition, provide appropriate time scales and priorities if needed.

- Always allow the individual to question an instruction, and provide a detailed answer – never allow an individual to engage in work when they do not fully understand what it is they are meant to do.

- Make sure all boundaries around acceptable behaviour and inappropriate behaviour are clear right from the start.

- Try never to allow an individual to leave work with any work-related stress or anxiety on their mind.

- Always have someone who the individual trusts available to speak to about worries at work.

- If possible have a clear beginning, middle and end to all tasks.

- Make sure time is taken to feedback as regularly as possible – daily may be appropriate in some situations. Feedback should be positive as well as critical.

- *Above all, have respect for the individual and their idiosyncratic way of doing things, do not judge or criticize simply because it does not adhere to the NT norm.*

These are just some suggestions of what may be helpful to some individuals, and I would regard all of them as reasonable adjustments. Naturally, some of the above will bear little or no relevance to many individuals – as unique and individual as each person is, so will the adjustments required.

As well as behavioural adjustments, there may need to be some environmental adjustments that can benefit a person with AS. Most people with AS will have differences in the way in which they process sensory information, and the problems that can come with this may be heightened at times of anxiety, stress or pressure. Thus, in a working environment, to fully support someone with AS it is essential to take sensory processing into account. As each person will be different in the way in which they process sensory information it is not possible to suggest the 'perfect' working environment in a generic sense. Suffice to say that it is often the sensory environment that can make the difference between the individual being able to work or 'failing' at their job. It would be unthinkable not to make adjustments to someone with a physical problem that required adaptations in the work environment – there is little difference between that scenario and someone with AS who, for example, cannot tolerate bright light. To those of you out there who genuinely want to employ individuals with AS, allow yourselves to be 'led' by the individual themselves. If someone says that they 'need' to work in isolation, in all probability that person does actually need to, rather than 'would prefer it'.

As well as sensory issues, it is advisable to always have somewhere that an individual can escape to as and when is necessary. Once again, however 'odd' this may seem, do not judge. If someone, perfectly capable at doing their job effectively, also now and again needs to hide away in a darkened room, then so be it. Most NTs seem to have their own, often more socially accepted, ways of coping – having cups of tea, stopping to chat to a colleague, making personal phone calls – a whole range of behaviours that lead to productivity when back engaged in work. Everyone needs to recharge their batteries now and again. The manner in which a person does this should not matter, so long as there is no harm to anyone. So many individuals with AS are denied the opportunity to work simply because their ways of coping are seen as odd or strange. Flapping or humming to oneself, for example, may lead to an individual being ostracized and singled out – even though this has nothing whatsoever to do with the ability to work (in most cases). By finding out what an individual needs to do to relax – even as simple as being on one's own – and allowing the individual the opportunities to do so can make a huge difference in the fight between meaningful employment and the benefits office.

On occasion the question is raised – should all individuals with AS be *expected* to go out and work? This is a tricky question to answer, and I am not sure there is a simple answer to it. Many individuals would like to work but are denied the opportunity – mostly through a lack of support or lack of appropriate adjustments being made in the workplace. Some individuals are able to work but end up developing secondary mental health issues as a result of the stress and anxiety they are put through at work. Some individuals are too anxious to contemplate work. And some may be content not to work. I think the more important questions are what is being done to fully support those who strive to work in enabling them to be successfully employed on a long-term basis? By successful I mean being a good employee while being fulfilled at work without suffering from discrimination, judgement or high levels of anxiety. What is being done to develop the necessary skills for those out of work who wish to be in meaningful employment? What is being done by employees to take on board the need for reasonable adjustments in order that individuals can access their employ? These are in desperate need of concrete answers in order that individuals are more able to gain and sustain employment.

Chapter 1: Employment for People with Asperger Syndrome: What's Needed?

Giles Harvey

Introduction by Luke Beardon

*Giles makes some excellent points in this chapter, and I am particularly interested in the way in which he matches up specific jobs that may or may not be compatible with the nature of AS. As he rightly points out it is not an exact science in any way. I sometimes get asked whether 'someone with AS' would be able to do a particular job – the answer is invariably, 'Well, it depends...'. The bottom line is that **nothing** is impossible in terms of the working environment, but much is dependent on all the variable environmental factors such as the knowledge of the employers, the physical working environment and what adjustments are put in place. In theory, there is no job that someone with AS would automatically be precluded from applying for. Obviously, on an individual basis there are a number of factors that will need to be taken into account; however, the notion that any particular type of job should exclude someone with AS just because of the nature of AS is irresponsible and inaccurate.*

Why is employment for people with Asperger Syndrome necessary at all, you might ask? The answer is quite simply this, employment not only allows people with Asperger Syndrome, but all people, access to friendships, money and well-being, and also occupies the mind. People who are working are less likely to be depressed and less likely to suffer from other health problems in later life, through lack of activity.

Unfortunately, while clear figures are not available, it is thought that less than 20 per cent of people with Asperger Syndrome are in work at any one time, and of those which do manage to find work, generally their jobs only last for short periods. It isn't uncommon to find people with Asperger Syndrome in their late twenties or early thirties with a chequered employment history of several low-paid jobs. These may have only lasted a few weeks, a few months or perhaps a couple of years. They may have been asked or forced to leave, and have large gaps of unemployment in their record. We know that in many cases this is nothing to do with lack of education, as Asperger Syndrome doesn't affect people's intelligence, and many people with Asperger Syndrome are of above-average intelligence. So that must leave other reasons for failure to remain in employment.

One principal reason, I feel, for many failures, is the lack of planning in the early years of education. You do not see people with cerebral palsy, diabetes, heart disease and cancer not taking the effects of their disability into account before looking for work. In my case the careers service was less than helpful, for I had no diagnosis of Asperger Syndrome in 1989 when I was initially looking for work. Indications that perhaps there was something different about me were never acknowledged: never once was any possibility put to me that certain careers might not suit me due to stress or lack of confidence. Only academic reasons for doing or not doing careers were ever discussed. Later on in life, on two occasions, I have asked for advice from the careers service and on both occasions I felt let down. On the first occasion I was told basically they couldn't help me and to come back when I was less ill, and was given a card for the Samaritans; on the other occasion all I was given was a list of academic careers that with my qualifications I might want to move into. On neither occasion were the limitations of having Asperger Syndrome ever discussed. If this has been happening on a wide scale for many years, perhaps we might understand why so many people with Asperger Syndrome are failing in their jobs.

The system with careers advice is that it obviously influences what young people go on to study in further and higher education and therefore, what career someone eventually does. You can't, in other words, split education from employment and perhaps in many government departments the two should be linked together at all levels. In the same way, if I didn't discuss education here first, we wouldn't be coming up with a full solution to this problem. Some moves have been positive in the United Kingdom, like the move to place careers along with other needs in education, including disabilities and special needs education, under the umbrella of Connexions for all those under the age of 25 with special needs or a disability. However, there is still much to do.

Many people fail to realize or even plan the effect higher education at a particular institution will have upon them. Some colleges work to a formal timetable and setting but many work informally. I have come across many young people who have left education without qualifications because they chose to study in the wrong environment. They have come out traumatized and never gone back into education. Worse still, sometimes they have never done anything else, but have sat around at home.

Higher education was certainly the best period of my life, to date. If all it took was to research into what the facility was like before I went, to ensure it was right for me, I would do so. However, many people fail to ask to look round colleges to see what happens, or fail to ask to visit during the day when the students are around. Neither do they find what the special needs departments can actually offer: at every stage you need to know what you're letting yourself in for, in order to survive and to make sure you are doing the right thing. No one with high-school qualifications should be sat idly at home without good reason.

Again, another failing that's perhaps down to the people with Asperger Syndrome themselves (and their careers advisors as well) is the choice of subjects studied at university. Many fail to work out if they might actually be able to use their skill for meaningful employment in the first instance, and if the career it leads to is suitable for a person with Asperger Syndrome. For example, consider space science. NASA only take on a handful of astronauts every year and universities have few lecturers in the subject, so why study it? In business studies, the business environment isn't suitable for those who can't handle stress or plan; no matter how good they actually are at the theory. Or perhaps a course playing the guitar interests you? In this case ask, is there any proper use for the skill at the end, what does it involve and what sort of work might it lead to? Playing the guitar can be pleasurable, but it's likely to be extremely low-paid employment and it's unlikely, unless you were really gifted, that you could make a full career out of it – or at least one you could live off! It would be better to study music generally as this widens your career options.

Another consideration is whether you could actually use the skill in relation to any physical attributes to the disability, e.g. acting may not be a good idea due to the pedantic way in which people with Asperger Syndrome speak, and the way in which they interpret and pronounce the written word. *[Editors' note: while some individuals with AS do have problems with prosody (voice intonation) many more have excellent mimicking abilities and enjoy and excel in drama.]*

If chosen correctly, subjects can lead to long and successful careers. Information technology, certain strands of science, accountancy, music and modern languages are prime examples.

One career we know people to be settled and performing well in is information technology, and the reason why is quite simple. Those in information technology often work on their own in a silent environment, and the role doesn't involve much direct face-to-face contact.

Some people, however, might decide they want to move straight into employment after school, and that's fine, but I would urge caution. Jobs which don't require qualifications are generally the aim of those people who perhaps messed around in school, and who enjoy joking around; people with Asperger Syndrome tend to be exactly the opposite of this. Therefore there is potentially a high likelihood of failure. At an unskilled level, we know employment which works best for people with Asperger Syndrome is in the large supermarkets where staff can have roles which do not involve interfacing with the public, such as positions like shelf stacking and working in the warehouses. In the United Kingdom, Royal Mail has had some success in employing people with Asperger Syndrome, due to its flexibility of roles and the simplicity of the jobs.

Jobs and careers of all types can be sub-divided into those which are, and aren't, likely to be successful, so that people with Asperger Syndrome and their carers and support workers know where the best types of places are to gain employment. In the table underneath you will see examples of some suitable and unsuitable jobs listed, as well as those which might be suitable for some but not for others. The list is, of course, by no means comprehensive. If anyone is using the book as a study tool they may wish to discuss these further, with a friend or support worker. You may also wish to think about the list alone by taking into account whether or not you have the right attributes, both in terms of qualifications and also social abilities required for the various jobs listed.

Table to show jobs which may suit people with Asperger Syndrome

High risk of failure	May suit some people but not others	Lower risk of failure
Any airport-based customer-facing roles	Lorry driver	Warehouse work
Air traffic control	Lecturer	Piano tuner
Armed forces	Librarian	Musician
Police officer	Warehouse work	Accountant
Fire officer	Decorator	IT technician
Mental health worker	Musical instrument instructor	Tourist guide
Bus driver	Nurse	Town planner
Train guard	Dentist	Funeral director/pall bearer
Salesperson	Primary school teacher	Gardener
Cashier	Factory worker (except target-based)	Postman
Secondary school teacher	Administrator	Web-site designer
Doctor	Receptionist	Van driver
Commission and target-based factory work	Careers advisor	Navigator and route planner
Waiter/waitress	Carer	Farmer/farm labourer
Taxi driver	Optician	Artist
Security work	Electrician	Photographer
Night club/bar worker	Plumber	Appliance engineer
Holiday rep	Window cleaner	Statistician

High risk of failure	May suit some people but not others	Lower risk of failure
Vet	Train/tram driver (non-fare collection)	Cleaner
Actor/actress	Mechanic	Academic researcher
Bricklayer/builder	Linguist	Crafts person
Driving instructor	Journalist	Magician
Ambulance driver	Bookshop worker	Milkman
Pilot	Fisherman	
Management trainee	Veterinary nurse	
Market researcher	Cook/chef	

Disclaimer: The above table is no guarantee that a particular career or job will or will not work for every person. The table has been provided in good faith and with the best knowledge of the author and various source material. Jobs vary and people vary in ability and anyone using this table as a resource to gain employment should be aware of this.

Why do the jobs in the high-risk category have a large risk of failure? Simply because of various different reasons in regard to the particular role. If the job involves dealing with tight deadlines, angry customers or very regimented settings and high levels of stress, or the fact that you need intuition skills and good body language reading skills to know how a person feels, then failure is highly likely. Those jobs in the middle category may suit some people and not others. Whether it suits someone's abilities or not depends on the type of thinking, be that lateral or literal, and also their ability to handle people in conflict situations. Concentration skills and abilities, or the nature of the location where the work actually takes place also need to be taken into account. Lower-risk jobs in the table above are not necessarily jobs that employees with Asperger Syndrome won't fail at, just that the odds of failing are much lower with most people who reside on the autistic spectrum.

At this stage I feel I ought to elaborate on my own employment history and what I feel could have helped along the way.

I never really searched for work while I was working my way through high school or college as the whole concept of work just simply scared me; I lacked confidence and the prospect of visiting several shops asking for application forms for casual work was just too daunting a prospect, although I knew others who did – and their confidence increased as a result. I did work for two summers, (prior to the introduction of a minimum wage in the United Kingdom) for the construction company my father worked for, for £60 per week during the college vacation. This always seemed to go fine without problems.

Later on, of course, I had experiences which were not satisfactory. My first such experience was between university courses where I had a period of nine months to fill. I went to see the local job centre's DEA (disability employment advisor). They found a job at a local mining machinery manufacturer, who had taken on additional work. Unfortunately, my skills did not match the position, yet for some reason I passed the interview and got the job. They wanted a speed typist; however, I am not a typist and so it resulted in me having to leave the job after two weeks. I later returned to university and gained a BA Honours in business administration. At this stage there were no specialist employment schemes so I decided, on my own initiative, to find a job that might be easy to obtain without much effort. Fortunately, at this time a new regional shopping complex opened and they decided to take all their staff on at a large open day. I was recruited as a cinema usher and offered two other job interviews on the self-same day. I took the job as an usher, which started within the month. Without support I lasted a mere 12 weeks: it was too hectic and at the end of the day I had to resign because the job was completely inappropriate.

I then didn't work for three years, until I started to work for the local autistic charity. I initially worked part-time and latterly in a full-time capacity. This lasted for three years and initially the set-up both there and through the employment agency I had at the time, was supportive. It then came apart, through staff changes, both in the organization and also within the supporting agency. This meant that the job drifted away from what I was used to and the support also drifted away! I couldn't cope with the ongoing changes, such as the new manager, and I was again in a position where I had to resign because the job was making me ill. I didn't work for around 18 months and was quite unwell during this period. Late last year I joined a new employment agency run by my local authority (council), and they found various work placements that eventually led to a job for a large haulage contractor initially for around 13 weeks. I am into my first few weeks and I am enjoying it: who knows if it will lead to anything more permanent? I have to look at the positives: the potential reference from a senior person at a large company, the experience with a large company and the fact this large company has customers with which the reference from a known person could potentially stand me in good stead for employment.

What might have helped and what problems have I come up against along the way?

There are several issues that I have had to face. Finding a job isn't easy and the more failure occurs and the more used someone gets to staying at home, the harder it becomes. So at all times I would advise you, where possible to try to find specialist employment advisors or schemes to offer support, which I do know exist throughout the United Kingdom. A brief look at the internet has also found sporadic evidence of support schemes in Australia, and I would therefore assume that similar schemes exist in the United States, Canada, Ireland and New Zealand. These schemes may range from Asperger Syndrome specific schemes such as NAS (National Autistic Society) Prospects in the United Kingdom, to more generalized schemes run by local authorities or other organizations. Currently, in the United Kingdom, a large push is taking place to get those described as long-term unemployed, back into the working environment, through various different schemes in different areas. If you live as I do, in the United Kingdom, the best person to approach is normally your disability employment advisor at your local Job Centre. Elsewhere, check who can influence access to any such schemes, and whether they exist; as a second port of call a health key worker like a social worker, for example (as in my case), can speed up referral to employment schemes. If there are known to be health benefits for a person gaining employment, it speeds up the wait from nine months to three months, once the referral paperwork has been filled in.

Avoid at all costs, if possible, having to sign on for Jobseekers' Allowance if this adds unnecessary pressure to find work which may not be appropriate. Incapacity Benefit is the better option if you qualify at assessment. Another technique which I have learnt, is to take up any courses the Job Centre is offering to gain employment. These can give useful tips on gaining work and build up confidence. Skills such as interview techniques and specific advice on how to sell your abilities (and also relevant hobby skills) to a potential employer in the best possible way, both at interview and in the application process, are invaluable.

One of the biggest shortcomings that people with Asperger Syndrome face, however, is the continuing advance of technology. In the UK, most office jobs will require a minimum skill of ECDL (European Computer Driving Licence), others will require competence in speed typing, and some may ask for ability in updating company websites. With the block on Goverment funding training for those who already have a degree, it would be a massive expense to me if I were to become proficient in those areas which are now considered vital. Those who have been working have been trained on the job. Many potential employees with a diagnosis of Asperger Syndrome fail to meet the requirements of posts being offered, because they are not up-to-date with recent developments and it is something the Government ought to be addressing as a critical issue, if its policy of returning to the workplace workers it regards as having disabilities is to succeed.

For me, whom I have worked with hasn't been the critical issue. Only when someone has consistently stood over me expecting me to make a mistake, have I become stressed and this is generally the issue with managers.

Try to avoid work in large corporate headquarters. In these locations there is an incredible level of stress placed on employees by the sheer nature of the amount of work dealt with, and the ruthlessness of the managers there. Senior managers do not allow failure and therefore a higher level of stress is placed on employees in the workplace. Most rules the company has will have to be fully followed in these locations, without error. They may also be much stricter about absence from the workplace, about team working and about punctuality.

Equally, some things help me to get through the day at work. Always have something to look forward to at the weekends: make plans. Always draw a clear line between work and home; the journey in my car is where my mind switches from work to home. If I am stressed after work because somebody or someone has said something, I might go for a walk to clear my head.

Another useful thing is to show your willingness to be part of the team, so to speak. Try to weigh up what people are like, be polite and give suitable eye contact. Try to make, where possible, some small talk, but not too much, for example 'Have you got anything nice planned for the weekend?' If someone's returned from holiday you might ask them if they had a nice time. Apart from that, remember the main and probably only reason the employer has hired you, is to do a job and that is what you should put most of your energies into. If your job is to bottle fizzy pop in a fizzy drinks works, that's what you are primarily there to do and that's the job you must learn inside out as quickly as possible, and nothing else. Well, almost nothing else! Sometimes an employer has a clause which says 'and any other duties'. This means if the employer, or a higher-level employee such as a supervisor, asks you to do something which you aren't used to, you do it. Normally these extra duties take place during training. If being trained, take a note pad and pen and jot down any notes on how to do the job.

If something is distressing, taking a break, going for a walk and calming down might help. Looking at work problems in regards to actual tasks; sometimes breaking the task into smaller pieces or mini-tasks can often help. Keeping a diary if the job role fluctuates or involves appointments in different places may also be useful, in order to record deadlines and times of meetings.

One issue I feel that has not been addressed is that of accessing promotions. Agencies are happy to get you into work, but less happy if you want a promotion. They tend to distance themselves or not be available. To me a job has a shelf life. When the job has expired you need to move onto something else. Very few people with Asperger Syndrome move beyond basic-level jobs. In order to meet someone with Asperger Syndrome's basic satisfaction and feelings of need, as with any neurotypical person, there is a need for promotion. This stage, however, can compromise the entire job if it isn't suitable as the job which was occupied has often been occupied by somebody else and quite often promotion leads to extra pressure. If a person isn't promoted, dissatisfaction with the overall job might lead to depression or a feeling of failure, and again the job fails. This is why it is important to have someone there to ensure smooth transition, for instance, allowing you to test the role before committing to it. A good idea might be for a company to allow someone to try the role while the current occupant of the role is on annual leave for example, and then to elevate the person if they manage the role successfully. Totally dismissing people's needs for progression, or not putting the infrastructure in place to allow this to happen as smoothly as possible, is not only failing the employee, but is also discrimination of sorts on the basis of disability.

Other useful advice I would give to people seeking work is to do as much voluntary work as possible. If you haven't worked for a long time it is vital that you demonstrate your skills, no matter how much it feels like a chore. Getting back into work has been one of the hardest things I have ever had to do, and each day has involved literal pain. Anybody expecting an easy ride should think again: it isn't, but you have to keep pushing, and with commitment things get better in the end and lead to fulfilment. Sometimes employers think the long-term inactive have no willingness or desire to work, so won't hire them. References from voluntary jobs or work placements can speak a thousand words, in that they open doors; they do demonstrate willingness and a desire to work. They may also show successful time management, the ability to do a task and to follow instructions, and so on. In fact, all the things a potential employer is looking for. Often placements can turn into jobs, if vacancies become available, and the person has been reliable.

Finally, some people might have a special skill or talent they believe they can sell to the outside world as a career. Sometimes, for example, I talk about autism; others might teach people how to play the piano, or drive a car or whatever. In these situations I would advise care and diligence, for many roles do not lead to any profit and for some people with Asperger Syndrome the prospect of building up custom might be far too daunting. If you are ill, the business effectively closes. Customers lose trust and walk away, and then it's an even harder job to re-establish your work. What I would therefore advise is ensure you research your target market properly, don't depend on anything like this as a first income, it rarely is. Ask yourself if you can cope with the people you might meet and their demands. Giving talks might be easy, but teaching a set of teenagers who don't really want to learn to play the piano, might be a whole different ball game.

You might also adapt a skill. As a good pianist you might seek work playing in a hotel lobby or for a ballet class, for example. Everything you do, however, must be registered with the relevant tax authorities. If you require the loan of any money, all banks will expect a full business plan with healthy projections or workloads or they will not offer financial assistance. Most banks or building societies will be able to supply copies of their business start-up guides, but I would advise setting up your own business only as a very last resort.

Summary of key points

1. It's vital to consider career options as early as possible – especially when making choices about subjects and courses while still in education.

2. Consider your skills and interests and choose a job based on what you are likely to be successful in and also enjoy.

3. When applying for jobs, it's important to look at aspects such as the size of the company, what tasks are involved, what skills you will be expected to demonstrate, and how you will manage your workload, deadlines, and so on. Once you have the complete picture, you will be able to judge how suitable you are for that job, and how suitable it is for you.

Chapter 2: The Job Needs to Work for the Worker

PJ Hughes

Introduction by Luke Beardon

As PJ so rightly points out, AS is something that affects everything that the individual does, including employment. AS is not something that can be switched on and off at a whim, however much an individual or those around them may wish otherwise. As a result of this it is essential that employers have a good understanding of the individual with whom they are working. What appears to be a common problem is that employers make assumptions, particularly based on an individual's 'performance'. If, for example, an individual has a productive day with no problems, it may be assumed then that the individual requires little or no support. If the individual then has a less productive day employers are often perplexed, and almost assume that it is deliberate in some way. This is not the case. Just as NTs will have good days and bad days, so will individuals with AS – but in the case of those with AS the effects may be far more damaging and severe than for an NT. Support then, for the individual, needs to be as flexible as possible; employers need to understand that factors outside of their control (i.e. outside of the working environment) may have considerable influence on an individual's anxiety and coping mechanisms. If an individual is in a highly anxious state then this needs to be taken into consideration within the workplace, otherwise the demands of the work in combination with anxiety levels could have a catastrophic effect.

Introduction

I was diagnosed with Asperger Syndrome in July 1999 and this was by complete accident. This is because my father was doing a ceiling job in a London hospital and was talking to one of the psychologists about me. It would seem apparent that the psychologist was asking relevant questions and then gave suitable directions for a diagnosis.

My employment history, with the exception of the Territorial Army, seems to fall very neatly into two parts either side of my diagnosis. By this I mean that the jobs I have had started and finished either before I was diagnosed or afterwards. I started in the Territorial Army before I was diagnosed and finished afterwards. My career appears to have quite a range of activities which involve both manual and office work. I have been employed in work which was essentially either stop-gap jobs, such as my vacation work, or existential, such as a number of jobs I have had after I have finished university; and then there have been those jobs that form an apparently obvious career path, such as working at a university. On reflection, it was lucky, in a manner of speaking, that I wasn't working when I was diagnosed because this gave be a bit of time to work out what to do next and where to go in life. I was actively looking for work as well, but being unemployed gave me a bit of time to put things into order rather more easily, i.e. no information overload!

There is also the job satisfaction value. For me, jobs have generally either been pretty high or pretty low in terms of satisfaction. The only jobs I have enjoyed to date are working in a hospital and at a university. These jobs, when I have looked back at them, seem to closely connect to my nature. Working in the hospital very strongly followed routines and structures. It was also a fixed hours job. Yet, working at university was complete flexitime. Obviously, this was as long as the hours I worked averaged out to what I was expected to work while fulfilling the obligations expected of me. These would be things like attending meetings (doing so with a suitable demeanour, including dress, and having a shower beforehand – even if it isn't my birthday!) and doing my job to the best of my abilities. Working at a university was really interesting and connected with interests and abilities of mine, especially at the time.

I have worked both fixed hours and flexitime (both true flexi and those with core hours). For someone with Asperger Syndrome, they both have their uses in terms of routines etc. This is because fixed hours provides, in our sense, an artificial structure, whereas with flexitime we can, within reason and in theory, have an input through our own natural routine. This area can be useful for reasonable adaptations because Asperger Syndrome doesn't just affect our working lives. Asperger Syndrome affects everything we do.

History

My first job was on a building site working as a labourer in the summer (about two months) of 1987. I worked fixed hours on a location in the London Borough of Bromley. I was clearing the rubbish the builders made as a result of their work and doing other odd jobs. At this point in time, I had just finished my A-levels (mathematics, pure and statistics, and physics). Because I didn't get the grades I needed for university, I returned to college to re-sit them. Once I re-sat them the following year, 1988, I got another summer job in Bromley working in a hospital bed-making factory. This was another job where I did bits here and there. I usually helped out in the latter end of the beds' construction although I did help out occasionally at earlier stages. Once I started university, I had vacation work both in the summer and at Christmas in a hospital. I was cleaning various wards, often together with another domestic. For a period of time, I was cleaning corridors as well. I worked during the day, but there were some evenings in which I did the same. This was probably the most routine-based job I have had because of the nature of the job, as I have just mentioned. I worked fixed hours, but also had certain structures within it as well because I couldn't clean the bathroom with the same materials as I would the ward kitchen. In the summer of 1991, the year when I changed course from physics and astronomy to statistics, I worked in an insurance company inputting various items of information. This was my first taste of flexitime. I can't remember if I had to work core hours in this job.

Once I had finished my full-time education, I had a mixed spell of unemployment and work. I didn't get a job straight after graduating. During this time, I raised money for a cancer hospital in Manchester until I was accepted onto a Graduate Workstart Programme in 1993. This was a job preparation course where the students developed skills for employment such as CVs and interview practice. There was also a job placement as well. I did mine at the Centre for Applied Statistics at a university between August 1993 and April 1994. I was involved in two fairly big projects in which I analysed a questionnaire from a local hospital and analysed data

about the failure of steel at high temperature from another local organization. While I didn't get a long-term job there (this was basically because I
needed postgraduate qualifications, which I didn't have at the time), I
stayed on to complete the projects I was doing. After this, I went to work
for a large private sector employer just outside Preston for three months
doing the same kind of work.

During the initial stages of the programme, we had our CVs looked at.
I remember one of the tutors making a note of the charity work I had done.
Retrospectively, it could have been better if I had followed this career path
at this time. But being pretty pigheaded, I wanted to follow the statistics
path at the time. It would be very interesting to see what would have
happened if I had chosen this path. It wasn't until I got diagnosed with
Asperger Syndrome and I revealed the diagnosis to a couple of people at
the centre, one of them suggested a contact at the Autism Research Centre
at Cambridge University that the autistic spectrum side (and, consequently,
disability generally) has become more of a possibility for work.

For the year after leaving above work, again in Preston, I was working
part-time in a pub collecting glasses, cleaning and dish washing in the
kitchen. I also did very brief spells at the local Post Office sorting letters,
around a Christmas period, and a couple of stints at the university at a
graduation ceremony involving collecting information for a questionnaire
and enrolling students. I then, through an agency, found work in an
alcohol-bottling factory. I worked there for a year before going back to
university for a postgraduate course in 1996.

In terms of my career, this is the point where I have completed everything I've done prior to my diagnosis. Over the ensuing few years
(between 1996 and about 2001), I feel was a transition period. This is
because I was diagnosed with Asperger Syndrome in July 1999 and over a
period of time I adjusted my life to this new information. Naturally, there
was all the panic of 'omigod', all the 'what ifs', and all that. Essentially, for a
couple of years I had a settling-down process where I did various courses at
a local college. These were courses that I have a strong aesthetic interest in,
which were A-levels in film studies and music and foreign languages
(namely, Italian and Spanish). I suppose this was a period of regaining a
base and discovering a new self. The only job that straddled both sides of
my diagnosis was being in the Territorial Army. I served for nine years,
between 1996 and 2005. I was mainly involved in Infantry Signals, i.e.
radio communications in an infantry unit. This was rather a mixed bag in

terms of Asperger Syndrome because certain aspects were quite natural to how my brain works, such as various procedures for assembling radios, lesson structures and so on. But there were aspects that weren't as natural, especially the social interaction and communication.

There are, so far, only two jobs that I have done since being diagnosed. That is working for two large public sector employers (2001–2004, 2004 to the present). Both jobs work flexitime but with certain, slightly different, constraints. Both of them have been basically data-entry jobs, although one also involves more administrative/office duties, such as letters and what have you. I am also involved with a disability sub-group in Sheffield and I am a committee member in the work-related Disability Support network.

Throughout my life I have done quite a lot of charity work through raising money. More recently, I have started 'working' in autism. I have undertaken numerous activities through giving talks and lectures, writing various articles, including a book, participating in research and attending various events, such as seminars and lectures (this includes qualifications in the autism spectrum). The vast majority of this work has been autism-specific events, mainly through the National Autistic Society and the Autism Centre at Sheffield Hallam University. My research participation has largely been at the Autism Research Centre at the University of Cambridge. I have also given presentations at diversity (i.e. general disabilities and other groups) events at work.

Retrospectively, the Territorial Army was quite interesting because its set-up seemed ambiguous for someone with Asperger Syndrome, well, certainly for me. On the one hand, the teamwork and communication style was not natural for me, whereas there were other aspects that were, even if they were in an artificial form. Here, I am referring to things like lesson structures and routines in the field (that is, sleeping in woods etc., rather than in barracks).

Where now?

My ambition now is to work in autism. My view is that being university-based in this area is, arguably, the way to go. Seemingly, the only real hazard is not having the qualifications and further (and, where necessary, relevant) experience to get going. This means that there is another difficulty of finding the money to get to the starting post for the qualification side. In terms of experience, I just have to keep an eye on what is happening. There is also continuing with the networking aspect as well. I have, in my opinion, developed some relevant skills since my diagnosis through gaining experience of giving lectures and talks as well as earning a Postgraduate Certificate in Asperger Syndrome. This has already been touched upon. In effect I have already obtained some of the qualifications and skills potentially required, although it is just a question as to whether they are relevant to the post I am going for. The challenge now is to widen and develop these skills in suitable areas. At the same time and in more general terms, it would be reasonable to assume that there would be associated careers. By this, I am referring to possibilities such as working in disability, or diversity, in general. I guess the more general area of disability is one where one may enter with a specialist background and consequently gain a more general one. Although I would have to find the right door to make my name even further. Realistically, it is important for me to build on and develop skills and experience whenever and wherever possible. This is where flexibility comes in. This is even though this area is not natural for me.

There are possibly other areas for me, which lie in statistics and languages. Whilst I don't think they'll be my main job, I suspect they'll be useful in whatever I do. After all, the statistics I have learnt will be useful for analysing data in research and languages are useful for media interviews and so on.

One hobby of mine in the past seems to be recurring at the moment. Loosely speaking, this relates to stage performances, currently as a musician (I play members of the guitar family, specializing in the classical guitar and the clarinet). I was a member of the drama society when I was an undergraduate student at university. I have an argument that this ties in with the speaking engagements I have so far given. This is because the bases of the various deliveries are principally the same; it is the content and intended outcomes that are different. After all, the music and the acting are intended for enjoyment, whereas the talks relate to a learning-based outcome. To be honest the theatrical life is something I am not planning to happen professionally, but I wouldn't mind it as a hobby. The 'serious' version, the talks and writing etc., is something I am more interested in.

Job support

Since I diagnosed, I have received support from an autism/Asperger-specific support agency run by a national charity. For me, they are most useful on the administrative side. By this I am referring to filling in job application forms. They also provide advocacy with employers. This is where they explain about the condition generally and how it affects the individual. I think it is difficult for any support team to give me support in general terms because I consider myself to be very independent. Having said that, I do think organizations such as this are useful for providing support where it is necessary. If there are times when I need to stress out or want to have a chat or whatever, I have a telephone number to ring. In this type of situation, I don't just have a support worker from the support agency; I also have contact with the Autism Centre at Sheffield Hallam University. The problem is that I get the impression that when support structures are in place, they are interpreted as being a hands-on approach. This, in my opinion, is a stereotype that should be abolished simply because I find this very ignorant.

I do get some reasonable adaptations. The main one in my current job in the Civil Service involves communication. Instead of using the telephone as an important form of communication, I use, as a main form of communication, emails and letters because this minimizes the effect of problems involving non-verbal communication. I have, however, used the telephone more often as I have become more used to the job. There have been times when I have had my emails checked before sending them off in order to make sure that they are suitable for sending. There was also a suggestion about using a rota system about staying until the office closes to the public. In principal, this may be a good idea, but one would have to consider other hazards as well. For me, taking time literally is the most obvious one. This means that if the rota system was implemented and there was a temporary increase of workload for whatever reason, then this could cause problems because I could have turned round and told my line manager that this wasn't my day for staying late.

Another method would be to look at other or additional ways of dealing with such situations. For example, implementing coping strategies for changes in routine, such as ways of appropriately stressing out. Action plans should be worked out by the relevant manager (or equivalent), support worker (if appropriate and/or equivalent) and, most importantly, in my view, the individual. After all, the individual will know what strategies work the best and, therefore, the remaining people should help in working out how best to implement such situations. In terms of job support, one could consider whether fixed time is better than flexitime or vice versa. I believe that both have their good and bad points. Idealistically, I would veer towards a combination of both. That is, having a flexible basis so that I can find my own natural rhythm within the job. There are, obviously, other factors to consider as well. The main problems with a predetermined fixed-time job is that I would get in and leave at the times described. And, in terms of leaving, this means that a job could remain unfinished at the end of the day. This can be an example of why I believe that it is important to be able to work with the condition rather than against it.

What I also think is useful is to consider is any obsession the individual on the autistic spectrum has and use it to develop potential career interests. Again, there may be support strategies that could be implemented for both the individual and the employer. For example, the work I have done so far on the autistic spectrum seems to be a contradiction to the rest of the jobs I have done. This is because this work has tended to be in the form of giving talks and lectures with a significant amount of writing thrown in, and there is direct communication involved through question-and-answer sessions during my talks. I have grown to feel comfortable with them through experience. The main explanation may be because of what the condition means to me and my obsession with it. Speaking of obsessions, I do think they can be useful for developing jobs and careers, as I believe that it is very likely that those on the autistic spectrum will be very knowledgeable about that particular area.

In general terms, I do a lot of self-support. This has basically come about through extensive reading and studying of the subject. This is because I can implement coping strategies that work for me best. Ultimately, I am the one, on a personal level, who has Asperger Syndrome and, therefore, the one who knows what works the best. Sometimes coping strategies may not necessarily be appropriate for the situation, but wherever possible I try and channel towards somebody I feel understands the best. These could be developed in reasonable adaptations at work. The only real criticism of support organizations, particularly if non-autistic people run them, is that while they may understand the subject, they don't know what it's like to have the condition. They may, however, have an autistic input, but I do feel there is a difference between living in autism and working in autism. Consequently, they can give advice about the overview of the subject as well as the individual aspects.

Earlier I mentioned independence. The truth is, I do not believe there is truly any such thing as real independence. After all, we all, to whatever extent, ask for advice for some reason from family, friends or whatever. It is also worth pointing out for whom the support is. There are some individuals on the autistic spectrum who do require significant support, others don't require as much. I believe that there is a need for support for people who connect to our environment. They could be work colleagues, the teaching profession and managers, amongst many others. Because this chapter is a work-based one, I am of the opinion that managers, the relevant ones more so, and work colleagues could do with support in understanding the autistic spectrum. Contact between the various groups is useful, arguably, in developing work skills for the multitude of autistic individuals.

General thoughts

There are, in my opinion, many difficulties that people on the autistic spectrum face in the workplace. After all, so many jobs want people with superb (I do realize that job advertisements suggest they are preferred) team-working skills as well as the same or similar levels of communication and flexibility. Guess what? These areas appear on the diagnostic criteria for the autistic spectrum as something to the effect of 'problematic'. Certainly, social interaction and communication do directly, but the material on flexibility also comes in the form of routines. I do recognize that the word 'preferable' does crop up and there are reasonable adaptations, but there are great big problems of how managers interpret this. There are organizations which I have already referred to, that can help provide direction on such matters. I would also involve the individual. The main hazards are that of communication and executive functioning (which essentially relates to making choices). This means that alternative methods of finding out may be required, such as observing what makes the individual anxious/distressed and happy instead of asking directly.

I do, however, think that there seems to be an improvement in understanding of the condition even though it is, in my opinion, in a transition period. I feel that the heart is there but actions are improving, or need to be improved. This may be because of a lack of understanding or fear of the unknown. This could lead to (possibly unfounded) negative beliefs. This is when fact-finding missions come in useful. I recognize that there will not always be time and so on. So this is where support groups are useful. This is because they can provide expert advice on the subject and they can come up with reasonable adaptations. I hope things like this will minimize controversy. At the same time, I recognize that there will have to be compromises; I believe that they will happen in time once both sides feel comfortable with each other. The problem is, who gets the proverbial ball rolling?

I believe that support systems in organizations are vital. I don't just mean having contact with supported employment schemes or any other support mechanism. There could be general disability committees/groups to provide information and support. I hope they'll have specialist connections so that more detailed information and support (and, therefore, advice) can be given. I am involved with such groups in the Civil Service. The biggest hurdle, in my experience and belief, is that while the heart and well-meaning are there for such groups in many organization, the action isn't working as well as it could be: they may not be used or used appropriately/seriously by the management system. This is a bridge that has to be crossed.

Generally, it has been a funny old life. What I have done in my working life has turned up quite a few surprises. Not all of my ambitions have truly been achieved, but many have been approximately there. As a child, I wanted to join the Army and be a meteorologist. Retrospectively, joining the Army was mainly because my maternal grandfather was an officer and I would argue that certain jobs (and careers) such as the Armed Forces are often what I call hereditary jobs because children often follow their parents into these jobs. This was achieved on a part-time basis through joining the Territorial Army. I have come close to becoming a meteorologist through unsuccessful interviews. My undergraduate qualifications would have certainly helped in getting that far. I then wanted to be a medical statistician. The closest was working at the Centre for Applied Statistics at a university. My current ambition is to work in autism. I am having some success in this, although there has been some expansion into general disabilities. To be honest, I was not originally expecting this. But, I have come round to the idea that it is also useful to put what I would naturally consider normal into a wider perspective. Sometimes it is great to come across things that end up as pleasant surprises.

The types of jobs that I hate the most tend to be those where I feel that I am simply existing. Examples include data-entry jobs. They are fine in short bursts, as stop-gap jobs, but are horrible when they seem to be long term. I like doing things that have a fruitful, satisfying outcome. I guess this is why something academic interests me. This is why one of the things I really enjoy about working in autism is being asked questions, I can take the time and consider them and then come up with an answer. The problem is such that there is rarely a single, definitive response. This means that I would have to suggest a range of ideas and possibilities. Sometimes I would have to admit that 'I don't know', but I hope to provide a point of contact that should be able to help. As much as I would like to provide definitive directions, the individualistic nature of the autistic spectrum makes it difficult. This is the challenge I like to have. This will also go for disability in general. In addition, I am a firm believer that autobiographical accounts, in whatever form they take, will give major clues to the answers because they provide the reality to the condition. In other words, our experiences are a vital part of understanding the autistic spectrum.

Summary of key points

1. Job satisfaction is of primary importance – it needs to be interesting and stimulating.

2. The job needs to work for the employee in all of its practical aspects. For example, is fixed time preferable to flexitime?

3. Support systems in organizations are vital, but they vary between organizations and generally still have some way to go until they are fully effective.

Chapter 3: Experiences of Employment and Stress Before My Diagnosis of Asperger Syndrome

Alexandra Brown

Introduction by Luke Beardon

Alex writes extremely perceptively about her experiences of employment. There are two points that seem wholly relevant to this subject that are within this chapter – first, the levels of anxiety and dread that employment can conjure, and second, the fact that if certain jobs were to become more AS friendly it seems likely that everyone would benefit.

Alex writes about how stressful work can be; people with AS should not be put in a position that their working lives cause major stress and anxiety at a level whereby their overall mental health is affected – and yet this is the reality for many people. The fact that they are not supported in the right way, or simply because people lack an understanding of what may cause stress, can lead to severe depression that can dominate their lives. Clearly this is not a situation that anyone should be put in, especially a population who have to cope with so many other issues at the same time. The sooner the general population develops a better understanding of how to interact with those with AS the better it will be.

The second issue that Alex writes about is how confusing some aspects of work are; lack of clarity in communication can lead to stressful situations where she is left unsure of what to do. This is not something that is specific to people with AS, however, so it would seem reasonable to suggest that clearer communication would benefit all employees, not just those with AS. As in education, changing practice to better suit those with AS will often (if not always) be beneficial to all involved.

I can remember, whilst attending primary school, being asked at various intervals, what would I like to be when I grew up? Most other people could come up with some sort of job they wanted to do, or even a person they wished to emulate, but I could never think of anything at all. I didn't like it when the teacher asked us this question, because it was just another area of my life where I didn't have a clue about what was going to happen. It didn't seem to matter to Richard that it was highly unlikely that he was going to be an astronaut, or to the teacher for that matter. It seemed that the most important thing was that you at least had some kind of idea or aim in life, however far-fetched it might be. I did try to come up with some ideas, but being a natural pessimist, I guess I was always very aware of my limitations and didn't see the point in considering anything that wasn't realistic. For instance, I knew that I couldn't be a Victorian engineer like Brunel, or a mountaineer like Sir Edmund Hillary or Tenzing Norgay, who were all people I admired. Later on I realized that it was highly unlikely that I would be able to follow a career related to my interests of dance and speedway. There were other factors to consider too, like would it be something my parents approved of, and would I be any good at it? I suppose you only really know about the jobs that the people around you have, or those of people you have heard of in the media; and I definitely knew I didn't want the kind of job that would draw attention to myself. So whilst most of the other children in the class seemed happy just to mention the first thing that came into their head or something related to the latest craze, I considered it to be a pretty important decision, and worried about what I might do when I grew up. I don't suppose it helps when you feel as though you have no particular talents and there is nothing you are particularly good at.

When I was 16, my mum decided that I ought to look for a Saturday job. The thought of having to get used to yet another new set of people and not knowing what to do petrified me. Wasn't it enough that I had just changed schools, and started trying to make friends and going out?

Obviously not; I should be like other people's children who were held up as a good example! I suppose my parents were only trying to help in some way, and thought it would do me good to be earning some money. I don't think I was lazy, I just found the idea a very daunting prospect. It took at least six months for me to find a job, during which time my mum brought home numerous application forms and encouraged me to go for interviews. I always felt relieved when I wasn't offered the job, particularly if it was something that really scared me, like working in a clothes shop in the centre of town. I didn't even like going in those places, with loud pop music blaring out and bright lights, full of chatting overexcited teenage girls. So I went for the next best thing – a check-out operator in a super-market! I'm sorry, but a free frozen turkey at Christmas was not an incentive or the selling point of the job for me!

I somehow managed to miss the induction day, and so when I arrived on my first day, it seemed like everyone else knew what they were supposed to be doing and I didn't. I remember feeling rather ill for the first few weeks and dreaded getting up on Saturday mornings. I did get used to it eventually, but I found break times a bit of a struggle. I sat with other girls my own age, but couldn't think of anything to say as I listened to them talking about boys and what they were going to be doing later that evening. Sometimes I found what they were talking about rather embar-rassing, or I didn't really understand what they were going on about. I suppose being quite isolated at school, I never got to hear what the other girls were talking about. So whilst I wasn't excluded this time, I didn't really understand or feel I could relate to their topics of conversation. I suppose what I did take from it, was the knowledge that I never wanted to attend an eighteenth birthday party, hen night or engagement party in my life.

I didn't especially enjoy working on the check-out because I didn't know what to say to the customers. It didn't seem enough that you checked out their shopping, some people expected you to chat to them. I noticed other people alongside me doing this, and the odd laugh, and I just knew I couldn't do it. When I go shopping I don't expect to be entertained at the check-out. Someone being polite and courteous is fine. I neither want nor expect anything more. Thank goodness for self-service check-outs! Worst of all was working on the deli counter because you had no idea what people were going to ask you for. Well, obviously you had some idea, because it had to be an item in the display cabinet, but if you only worked there once every few months, you had no idea. The café was a bit of a nightmare too, because I never knew which customer had ordered the meals I had to take out from the kitchen, and being very self-conscious, it was a painful experience having to call out people's orders. I think my favourite job was stocking shelves when it wasn't busy. I enjoyed being on my own and making sure everything was stacked in a neat and orderly manner. I can't say I was too sorry when the time came for me to leave.

Whilst on holiday from university, I had a few summer jobs, one of which was working as a field worker on an archaeological dig, which I did for a couple of summer holidays. I found the work very interesting, and was able to see how the work I was doing fitted into the picture as a whole. I dug down to a certain layer, cleaned up the area using a trowel, drew a plan using a planning frame and grid paper and marked the different levels on the plan using a theodolite; then pictures were taken and the planner transferred my plan of the area I had dug up onto the main plan of the site. Although I liked the job itself, the best memory I have of the first year is that it was probably the first time in my life that I felt settled and happy without any anxieties and doubts creeping in, because I met a group of people who liked me and appreciated me for being the way I was. We lived in tents in an orchard next to the priory where we were working, sur-rounded by woodland and hills, totally isolated from everyone and every-where else. So whenever I felt the need, I could wander off and be by myself, or I could be with other people if I wished.

When my daughter was younger, I enjoyed helping out at the small village primary school that she attended, working with individual children and small groups. I found this very rewarding and decided that I would like to go into teaching. On reflection this was not the best idea, but it seemed a good idea at the time. I suppose I was quite lucky getting a full-time teaching job straight after I finished my course. However, as soon as I found out I had been given the job I began feeling anxious. I started not being able to sleep, and I couldn't join in any family activities or even hold a conversation with members of my family because I felt so stressed out about it – and this was two months before I started the job! I lasted about 18 months, and other than to say it was one of the most stressful experi-ences of my life – where I couldn't eat, sleep, think or participate in family life – I still find it too difficult to say much more than that. I felt terrible that I had let everyone down, because my partner and daughter had made a lot of sacrifices so that I could study for my Postgraduate Certificate of Education (PGCE), both in financial terms and the way in which I had neglected my family; and then there was the emotional support I required whilst I was working. I also felt like a complete failure, and it has taken me several years to realize that there were some aspects of the job that I was very good at, but I was only able to focus on the negative points at the time. At the same time, I felt utter relief at the fact that I no longer had to put myself in this stressful situation any more, and it felt good to be able to eat and sleep and make time for my family again.

With hindsight I can now see why I found certain aspects so difficult, and I wonder to myself, why did I choose to work in schools? I hated school as a child; it caused me so much stress and unhappiness, what on earth made me think that it would be a good idea? I suppose I know the reasons why. Some members of my family thought I would make a good teacher because I liked children and could be very patient with them. I guess I enjoyed helping out in school; I also had a part-time job as a pupil support assistant prior to and whilst studying for my PGCE, and thought I could make a go of it. I suppose there were warning signs and aspects that I found difficult, but I put them to the back of my mind, and thought that I would somehow miraculously be able to deal with them when they arose. What I now know is that these were issues that I don't think I could ever overcome, because they were simply things that I am incapable of doing, and always will be. At least now I know why I had the problems that I did, and I hope I can try and avoid them in the future. I think I find it difficult to admit defeat sometimes, or at least I can't bear the idea of having to give in, or failing at what I am doing. I guess it has something to do with commitment to a certain extent, and once I have committed myself to something, unless I am made to give up, I keep going. I think when you work really hard and try your best, and it just isn't good enough, it is very hard to deal with. I know that I take any type of failure or criticism very badly, but looking back, I can't believe how I kept going for so long.

Sometimes I hate my current job, but then again, there are some aspects of it that make me feel that I am very lucky to be working where I am. I now work for a school library service, so I am able to use my knowledge of education and children in my work, and I really do feel privileged to be able to spend my time amongst so many books about so many different subjects. I was very apprehensive when I first started, but I found everyone in my department to be quiet and friendly, and although I felt a bit anxious about knowing what to do and what was expected of me, I realized that it was within my capabilities, and was soon given more challenging and varied work to do. At this point in time I really enjoyed my job and looked forward to going to work. I sometimes brought work home with me, because working out statistics in my spare time seemed like an enjoyable thing to do. I think that because I demonstrated I was proficient, and that I was conscientious, I was given additional work to do, well above the scale I was employed on. I was quite happy with this, because even though it was sometimes a bit stressful, I felt justified in saying that certain tasks hadn't been completed because of the amount of work I had been given to do, and this was understood. I found that because I felt settled and secure, or more to the point, I felt like I was doing my job well, I was happy and able to solve problems without having to seek reassurance from other people. I think I reached a point where I knew what was expected of me, I was aware of when it was acceptable to seek guidance and didn't feel awkward in doing so. I even managed to conquer my fear of using the telephone, at least in a work context. At first I had to make quite detailed notes about what I was going to say to people on the phone, but as I became more knowledgeable about the service I found that I was able to answer queries and talk to people when it was work related.

Another positive point seems to be that I apparently know which option each school subscribes to in our region out of approximately 400 schools. This can actually be quite useful at times! When a colleague a couple of scale points above me retired, I was asked to deputize initially, and then was interviewed and appointed for the post on a temporary basis only, as the whole of the library service was about to undergo a major change. I thought that I would be given the job because I knew I had demonstrated that I was capable, but even so, with five other applicants, it was not a foregone conclusion. I was pleased when I found out, but I wasn't surprised because I felt like I had worked hard and was definitely capable. Unfortunately, all good things come to an end! The library service, along with other public services, underwent a rather radical change. First, I had to reapply for my job because I had only been appointed temporarily. I remember commenting to my line manager that I would be no good at managing people, and she replied that she hoped that I would be. I didn't understand at the time the significance of her comment. I'm not sure whether I didn't read the new job description properly, or whether I just didn't understand it, but it certainly came as a shock to find that I was line-managing five other people. It wasn't a very happy atmosphere at this time because lots of people, including myself, were having to reapply for their own jobs, or were being moved around. I was really nervous about being interviewed again, and on the morning of the interview, my boss came and told me that she didn't feel that the other applicants scored anywhere near as many points as myself, and so there was no need to go through the interview process.

From here on in it all seemed to go downhill. I found that in addition to my previous responsibilities I was expected to take on more of a managerial role. I was able to undertake appraisals by strictly adhering to the guidelines, and I took this matter seriously, as I wanted the people I worked with to feel like they could have their say, and have the opportunity to make decisions about their role in the organization. I think that the major problems I have encountered have been related to communication. Quite often I am not given specific instructions, so I am not always sure about what I am supposed to be doing or what I am supposed to be taking from a certain situation. Sometimes I am asked to attend a meeting and report back to the department. So I attend the meeting and I am not sure what is relevant. I start off trying to remember everything that is being said, and after a while I can't remember any of it, or because I don't have anything specific to listen out for, I go off into a daydream, and suddenly I realize that I have no idea about what is going on and feel panicked into remembering anything at all, just so that I have something to report back. Consequently, few people in my department have any idea of the information discussed at such meetings. I feel bad that the other people in my department may not always know about changes that are occurring, or new procedures that are being implemented, because either I have not been made aware that I am supposed to pass this information on to my colleagues, or I am not even certain whether I have received the information myself. There seem to be so many different layers to management within the organization, and information is to be cascaded down to a certain level, but it often seems unclear to me who is supposed to know what. Another problem I have encountered is the fact that if your line manager is uncertain, and they pass the information down to you, it seems to become more and more unclear. Maybe other people don't see it like this, maybe it makes sense to them, but I like to fully understand something before I pass it on to someone else, because how can you answer any questions about it or implement it if you don't really have any idea what it is about? Sometimes my line manager and boss ask me to find out certain information for them, and they seem to presume that I can go and find this out with only the vaguest idea of what it is they are wanting. Quite often I am uncertain about what I am trying to find out, so I relay what I think the query is to the relevant person, and hope that they have an idea of what I am talking about. Then if they ask me any questions I have to go back and find out the answer, and I feel pretty stupid.

My own difficulties with communication have also created problems. For instance, if someone at work asks me where a particular file is located, sometimes I have to physically show them where it is, because I am not able to explain it to them, even if it is fairly simple to find. I can't seem to find the right words. I end up trying to point at it, and then having to take them to the item concerned. Or, if the caretaker brings up a parcel, I am unable to describe where it needs to go, and so ask him to leave it with me, because it is easier to do it myself than try and explain to someone else. Consequently, I end up with loads of things to sort out which someone else could and should have done, but as I am unable to communicate to the other people what I want doing, I don't have much choice, and this places me under more stress.

Other problems that I have encountered are the fact that I don't know when I am being told something for my information, or whether I am supposed to act on it in some way. So on numerous occasions my boss has told me some information, and sometimes I remember it because I think that it is relevant, but other times it simply goes over my head because I don't recognize how it is of use to me. Then when I am asked if a certain task has been completed, I have to say no, because I have no idea what I was supposed to be doing. Sometimes I have to admit to my boss or line manager that I don't have a clue what they are going on about, and sometimes I pretend I know, but then panic, because I am not really sure what needs doing. We are given such a lot of information. It would be helpful to know which are the really important and relevant bits, or to be told that they want me to do certain things. It was puzzling, before I knew I had AS, to realize that I should have done something, but seemingly knew nothing about it; but now I am aware of what is happening, it is worse in some ways, because I am forever wondering if I should be doing something, or whether I have missed something. Other times I try and listen, but I haven't concentrated on what is being said, or the instructions aren't specific enough, and then I worry because I don't know what I am supposed to do. I think that because I am employed on a certain scale I should instinctively understand what is being asked of me. In the past, when people from other departments have asked me if I am aware of certain issues and policies, I have had to say no, the information hasn't been passed on to me. However, in some instances it may well have been, but as I was not aware that the information was relevant or applied to us I haven't taken it in, and as far as I am concerned I never received it in the first place. So maybe I am doing other people a disservice and making it look like they haven't passed on the information, but it isn't intentional.

Another problem is when people are indecisive – even though I am myself. For instance, sometimes my boss will ask me to do something, and part way through she will change her mind or change some of the details, and I go away not having a clue what I am supposed to be doing. I used to think that I should be able to work these things out, but now I will sometimes go and say I'm not sure what she's asked me to do, and ask to go over it again. I guess in some ways I have more of a problem with people from other departments, because I don't feel confident enough to ask for clarification from them. Sometimes this kind of thing gets me down, and is frustrating for myself, and presumably the other people concerned.

One of the greatest difficulties I have had to face is dealing with people. I am expected to show job applicants and new members of staff around the building and introduce them to other people, resolve staff issues, and even arrange Christmas meals. I don't know which has caused me most distress, but I know that the period leading up to Christmas was especially difficult. To start with, people seemed to assume that I should organize a Christmas meal, and for someone who hates dining out, using the telephone and socializing, I found it almost unbearable. In the end I had to pretend that I didn't hear people discussing what we might do right in front of me, and tried to avoid contact with anyone else. Things got so bad that I had to isolate myself at home, and I spent my weekends lying on the bed unable to move or open my eyes because it hurt so much. I felt very angry at work because I didn't want to go to a Christmas meal, let alone organize one. It isn't on my job description, so I resented the fact that it was expected of me.

I know that there have been certain incidents, which probably seem like nothing to most people, that really upset me, or I dwell on them and don't know how to handle them. Like, if someone that I line-manage breaks a minor rule, I am not sure what to do; because if it is a rule, then I should say something, but I feel awkward about doing so. Partly because

I'm not always exactly sure what the rules are, and partly because I find it difficult to speak to people and decide which is the best way to approach the matter. It probably seems like nothing really, but having to deal with this kind of thing makes me really unhappy, and I feel like I can't do it. It makes me feel really inadequate and pathetic not to be able to deal with these kinds of situations, which in turn makes me feel more unhappy. I just don't know what to say to people and how to deal with their reactions. If you ignore things though it just causes ill-feeling and things invariably get worse.

The thing is I'm not bothered if people don't like me, if I know I am being fair, and doing my job effectively. I don't want to do or say things to make myself popular with the people I work with. It's when I am not doing my job well. I mean obviously it's not nice if people don't like you, but if they think things are unfair or you are inconsistent, you can understand that; the reason it bothers me is because I know they have a valid point and I am more upset about my inability to be able to do my job properly.

Looking back, I'm not really sure how I managed to get through the Christmas period. I know I did a lot of crying, a lot of hurting myself and withdrawing from everyone at home. I considered committing suicide again, and felt very angry. I found myself crying on the way into work and feeling extremely anxious walking into the building. I hoped that people would just leave me alone and not talk to me. The atmosphere in the building felt stifling and my sense of hearing seemed to become hypersensitive, especially to other people's voices. I couldn't bear hearing other people talking; it made me feel angry and made my ears hurt. The lights seemed to become far too bright, and I found that the only way to make being there more bearable was to walk round with one of my ears covered with my hand, and it seemed to take the edge off the noise and brightness. It seems to make you incredibly tired. One time when my boss was away, I went into her office at lunchtime because I couldn't bear to listen to or see anyone else, and I lay down on the floor behind her desk and curled up and closed my eyes. It took a while to feel calm, and then I nearly fell asleep. When you return to work, the anxious feeling returns and your instincts tell you to get out of there, but you know you can't. I think it's the hopelessness of the situation that gets to you. It feels unbearable, but you've got to be there and there's nothing you can do about it.

Now, at lunchtime, I take a book and sit in the car. I feel like I need to get away from everyone, and there doesn't seem to be anywhere in the building where I can do this. Sometimes I read, but if I am feeling particularly stressed or tired, I curl up on the back seat and close my eyes and try to shut everything out. Sometimes I just see darkness, and sometimes I imagine I am somewhere else, or I try and think about happy memories. Often I drift off and am suddenly aware that I was almost asleep, and my time is up.

I guess one of the things that really bothers me, is that if I did decide to find another job, I wouldn't want to leave this one feeling like I have failed. That's pretty much how I view what happened last time. I didn't feel too dishonest holding back certain information when I started this job, because the parts of teaching I was good at were the ones relevant to my current job, so I guess I was just being selective with what I chose to tell them. If I do get another job in the future though, I want to know that I left everything in good order, with all loose ends tied up, so to speak. Most of all, I don't want to feel like I have failed at it and that I can't be completely truthful about which aspects I was good at and the parts I found more challenging, because it is pretty much unbearable. I think what really upsets me, is the fact that when I was younger, I held out the vague hope that things would get better as I got older. I think I believed that when I was grown up and working, I would have more control over things.

I'm now 37 years old, and have been aware that I have AS for about 12 months; and I have decided that it would be beneficial for me to get a diagnosis in terms of work. I think if I were to look for another job now, I would make sure I read the job description very carefully, to ensure that there were no aspects of the job that I would feel uncomfortable with. The last few interviews I have attended, I pretty much anticipated all of the questions they asked, by working through the job description and person specification systematically, and I looked up information related to the post. Matters were somewhat brought to a head in my current job, when I was asked to attend a training course in which I felt I could not possibly participate. Following much encouragement from my partner and a friend, I told my boss that I am undergoing an assessment for Asperger Syndrome. I can't say that things have got much better just yet, or that I am enjoying going into work; but I am hoping that there may be some positive changes. My boss has started to give me more specific instructions, and to write down tasks and queries for me, which helps. I think the major difficulty will always be the people management side of things. I can't see myself ever enjoying or being comfortable with this aspect of my work. I would like to stay where I am if at all possible, because people seem generally accepting of some of my ways, like skipping and galloping along the corridors at right angles, and some of the things I say; but if I have to change jobs, I hope I will have more of an idea about what is suitable.

Chapter 4: 'How Do You Communicate that You Have a Communication Problem… When You Have a Communication Problem?' Asperger Syndrome and Employment

Neil Shepherd

Introduction by Luke Beardon

Neil is an exceptional writer – his sense of humour is superb, as is his insight. One thing that really strikes me is his advice on communication, and how really listening to the individual is crucial. Much of the NT population think and process information in a way markedly differently to those with AS. As a result it can often be extremely difficult to understand things from a different perspective. Although I strongly advocate the development of a better understanding of AS by the NT population, I also think that accepting the reality of an individual's perspective is critical. Too often an individual simply will not be believed. As Neil notes, the reaction of 'Well, everyone feels anxious sometimes' or even 'I think we all are a bit autistic' is less than helpful. To suggest that the 'average' NT can simply empathize to a great extent to with a person with AS is simply not accurate. To suggest to someone with AS that this is the case can be demoralizing, and should not be done. However, simply taking the time to listen to an individual's experience and accepting that it is an accurate representation of their perspective is a valuable way forward. However difficult it may be to believe (especially if you have already made assumptions about the person) it will almost invariably be true. Acceptance is the first major step forward in the way towards mutual collaboration.

Introduction

Hello. First thing I'd like to do is thank you for picking this up. Maybe you're interested in Asperger Syndrome (AS) and employment, maybe the pretty cover drew you to it, or maybe you're standing in a bargain book emporium trying to waste a bit of time. Whatever the reason, you picked this up and this instantly qualifies you for a cash prize.[1]

The way I see it, you probably fall into one of the following categories:

1. An Aspergic person looking for/starting work.

2. An Aspergic person already in work, looking to find out how other 'Aspies' cope.

3. An academic looking for an insight into my bizarre little world.

4. An employer wondering about employing/dealing with an Aspergic person.

5. My mother.

6. None of the above.

With the exception of (5) and (6) we'll hopefully go on a voyage of discovery through the wild and wacky world of AS and employment and find out what actually happens when 'AS' meets 'work', what the benefits, problems, rewards and challenges are – I hope from both sides of the 'employment bridge'. You're probably wondering what qualifies me to write about all this (and if not, well done you for putting your trust in me). I'm

---

1   Cash prize not available to persons living or dead.

not a fancy professor with most of the alphabet after my name (I do have some letters but they've got nothing to do with AS, psychology or even anything remotely related), I'm not an expert in my field and I'm not even sane most of the time. What I am, though, is someone who's been there and done that. I'm just a regular guy who found out he was Aspergic pretty late in life (31 years after first popping into the world). Someone who's seen and experienced the workplace both as a 'norm' and as an Aspie. I've battled, struggled, questioned, worried, stressed and seen what does and doesn't work, how people react, where 'problems' can arise and how best to either avoid or solve them. This might not be a definitive work on the subject but it's written by a 'front-line' person. So, strap yourself in, we're about to start writing properly (with big words etc.).

Is it worth it?

If you step out of your Aspergic world, be that your own skewed perspective (if you're an Aspie), your research institute or whatever, if you mention 'Asperger Syndrome' to someone you'll probably be greeted with a blank expression. You might get a bizarre response (I know that one woman I told replied with, in all sincerity, 'Oh my God, that's terrible – how long have you got left?'). The fact is, 99.99 per cent of people will never have heard of Asperger Syndrome and they don't know how to respond to it, what it means, how it will affect them – this is exactly the same in the workplace and immediately presents a challenge both for the Aspergic person looking for work and anyone who finds themselves faced with employing them.

The fact that you're even reading this diatribe of gibberish means that your 'cosy little world' is probably about to have the added bonus of AS meeting employment, in one way or another. If you're an Aspie looking for work then good for you – you're about to enter an even more exclusive part of an exclusive club (the stats say that only 12 per cent of us manage to hold down full-time employment). You're going to enter a new world, earn money, meet people, do what you don't want to do, learn new skills, challenge (and I hope beat) things that you find hard, and I'm not going to lie and say that it's going to be easy as it won't be – it's definitely worth it though and it can, actually, be fun. If you're an Aspie already in work then you probably already know what I'm talking about – the challenges, the reactions from other people, the opportunity to expand your world and push yourself to new limits.

Then there's the 'flip side' of the scenario and you could be the employer having to deal with an Aspergic employee. Just as it's a big thumbs up to the Aspie looking to start work, well done to you for looking beyond the 'usual' and even considering someone who isn't 100 per cent 'normal' (and believe me, 99 per cent of 'normal' people most certainly aren't 'normal'). Employing an Aspergic presents a whole new set of challenges but the benefits can be tremendous. You want employee loyalty? You got it. You want precision, honesty, punctuality, dedication? You got it. You want an employee who will gladly join in and be the life and soul of the party? Err, let's just 'pass' on that one for now.

Every Aspergic is different and that's simply down to the nature of the condition. While one Aspergic might be loud and never stop talking, others (like me) barely say two words and the traits and 'symptoms' do vary from one person to another. How these elements affect the work environment, naturally, is different in each case but one element that is just about common for all Aspies is communication. The modern world relies so much on communication and it is at the core of many businesses or, at the very least, forms a vital part of their business. Whether it's serving people on a check-out, discussing ideas with colleagues, visiting customers, presenting sales forecasts to the managing director – the need for communication is paramount. It's also the biggest stumbling block for Aspergics (as Aspies will already know and employers will quickly discover).

How you face that challenge depends on how you approach it, how much you're prepared to let it rule your life, and the level of support and help that employers are willing to provide. Legally, and I hate having to go down this route, employers can't discriminate against disabled people. How well adhered to this is though is another matter (and one that I'm not commenting on) but, in my experience, most of the 'reluctance' to help can be solved through educating people and making them realize that, just because you have needs that are different to 'normal', it doesn't mean that employers have to make radical changes. You, as an Aspie, thought you were just getting a job when in reality you were actually getting two: your actual job and that of teaching the unclean masses what AS actually means.

Getting the job

I don't want to go into great detail about the formalities of getting a job as this is not an Aspergic-specific problem (and there are plenty of guides to help you through that particular minefield). There are things that Aspergic people and employers do need to consider though, and the biggest problem that I've found is whether the Aspie mentions it or not to their potential new boss. If you mention it and don't get the job, then was it because of the AS? Do you, alternatively, keep quiet and then 'announce it' once you start (basically, hide the fact)? Discrimination doesn't (or shouldn't) exist but how true this is is questionable (you don't actually *have* to reveal it so that can be a nice 'get out' clause). The only advice that I've ever been given on this is to, however tough, rely on feelings – if you feel that you want to tell the interviewer then do it (but I usually make sure I've got a swathe of 'positives' to reel off just in case). You can look at this another way: if you don't feel that the interviewer can accept your announcement, it doesn't bode well for actually being able to work with them (so think of it as a warning sign about taking the job).

So how should you react if your potential candidate announces that he/she/it is Aspergic? I might sound as though I'm preaching from the 'good book AS' but don't simply dismiss Aspergic people. They were good enough 'on paper' for you to want to interview them and, as has been mentioned before, there can be major benefits to employing an Aspergic. It might not be an easy ride, you might hit all sorts of problems (both with your new 'Aspie' and with your existing staff – some people can be, sometimes unexpectedly, very blinkered and ignorant) but, as I know from bitter experience, people (on both 'sides') *will* adapt, issues *will* resolve themselves and you'll end up with a highly efficient member of staff who will baffle, astound, amaze and repay you many times over. Trust me, Aspergics are worth the effort. Besides which, Einstein, Newton, Michaelangelo, Beethoven and even Bill Gates (amongst others) are all suspected Aspergics – do you really want to pass up the an opportunity to employ the next Albert Einstein?

The 'problem' areas

I've worked full-time for ten years now (it seems a lot longer though - something in the region of about a thousand) and have experienced a lot of different environments, people, working conditions, attitudes and situations. I also know what's tripped me up, what's caused me problems and, to a certain degree, what I can and can't do. Knowing your limits is important not only to avoid putting yourself into stressful or difficult situations but also to be able to push yourself (i.e. measure whether you've 'improved') and, even more importantly, inform other people about what you can/can't handle.

You could read the last bit of that statement and think that you're drawing a line in the sand where work is concerned but I don't want it to come across like that. My boss has learned (eventually) that group situations scare me to death, and cause me to get very stressed and upset (other things do too but you get the idea). He knows what my limit is but he also knows that if he structures a situation properly, gives me enough warning and allows me time to prepare myself, I can probably cope. He never orders me to do these things but he asks and makes sure that I'm comfortable, and he's able to do this because I know what my limits are and I've been able to explain to him what my limits are. Sometimes I can't do it (depending on the circumstances, group dynamics etc.), sometimes I have to bite my lip and live with the anxiety (often amazing myself at how well I cope). I'm at that 'line in the sand' and, maybe only briefly, I've stepped over it. If I'm OK then I can draw a new line, if not, I can scurry back to safety. Basically I'm testing myself, pushing my limits and expanding and building my abilities – according to the internet, this is called 'life'.

I'm lucky in that my boss understands. Actually what I should really say 'my boss understands *to a certain degree*'. It's taken a long time to reach this stage and at times he's been exasperated, dismissive and, no doubt unintentionally, made life very hard for me and been totally unable to understand where problems lie or how to solve them. I'm a tenacious [insert rude word here] though and, having suffered from depression far too many times in the past, have refused to let life at work get me down again. Whether by design or pure luck, I'm here, I've got a 'problem' and I've got to deal with it…and that means it's time to educate the heathens. Sorry, I sound like some sort of 'preacher'.

I was diagnosed with Asperger Syndrome while I've been in my current job (which probably makes you ask how do I wonder about whether to mention it at interview or not – let's just say that it's nice to have a 'day out' occasionally) (should I leave that in? Oh what the hell, no one at work will ever read this – half of them can barely walk upright) and it has been a very bumpy ride. There have been 'incidents', flashpoints, misunderstandings and, after an awful lot of work, people are finally understanding and accepting the situation and me.

How did I do it? Did I wave a magic wand and make everything suddenly 'right'? Did the knowledge fairies magically make everyone understand? Of course they didn't and the reason that this didn't happen all boils down to one very simple fact: people don't care.

That might sound like a very sweeping and cruel statement but it is actually true. Following my diagnosis I became obsessed with AS (blimey, an Aspergic who's obsessed about something, that's certainly never happened before), became depressed and complained that no one was understanding or caring. My boss, quite bluntly if truth be told, asked me why everyone else in the office should? If you think about it, there's no reason why they should care or understand. At this time the 'company' (as in management) knew but it wasn't 'public knowledge' so the immediate response to this situation would simply be down to one of people not knowing the situation. OK so we'll just tell everyone – simple solution and the job's done.

I was all for going down this route but two things stopped me. First, I'd told everyone in my little IT department (three other programmers, a supervisor (my boss), and the head of department) what the situation was as soon as I'd been diagnosed (via email of course – couldn't actually talk to someone face to face). I explained that AS wasn't contagious, I wasn't suddenly deranged (I'd actually always been deranged and that it had nothing to do with being Aspergic), when I didn't look them in the eye I wasn't being rude etc. The response was... 'interesting'. To a certain degree I did become 'contagious' as what little interaction I'd had before totally disappeared – I was isolated and exiled by most of the department. Second, the head of department, who was smart enough to realize that I *wasn't* contagious, then tried to downplay my 'traits' – 'Oh everyone gets anxious', 'We're all bad at talking to people' etc. You can see what he was trying to do but it was actually the polar opposite of what was really needed. If you look at AS from a totally logical point of view, a lot of the 'problems' are merely the same as those experienced by 'norms'...but with AS they're intensified to such a degree that they cause a level of anxiety that is well beyond 'normal' (or acceptable). Yes everyone gets nervous when they have to make a speech (for example) but imagine that nervousness amplified a million times. The 'everyday' stresses and strains that people deal with without realizing it can easily become massive barriers for Aspergics. The best example of this was when I explained that even going to the men's room is tantamount to a military manoeuvre for me – got to check where everybody else is, make sure that no one is about to walk into the department (just in case I bump into them), check that I have my mobile phone with me, is my work saved etc., etc., etc. When people realize that you live with this kind of thing going on inside your head, they look at you as if you're mad but it's this level of understanding that most people just don't have.

The second thing that stopped me sending a company-wide email was the advice that my boss gave me. He explained that, quite rightly, nobody (i.e. most people outside the Asperger's 'club') has actually heard of Asperger's. Yes some might have heard of autism but, even then, it doesn't affect them so why should they spend any time thinking about or considering it? In my Aspergic little head I'd logically deduced that people needed to be informed…so inform them. The fact that people wouldn't take this information onboard or would fail to be as obsessive about it as I was never occurred to me. Thinking 'outside the box' is something that most people fail to do…but why should they? The world, including the workplace, is built and designed around the majority (as it rightly should be) and most people simply fail to realize when people are having a problem or are disabled (unless they're somehow physically disabled).

Faced with situations like this you start to gain a new appreciation of how 'normal' people think – they don't understand but, at the same time, why should they? Chances are they'll never meet another Aspergic (or maybe even autistic) person again so why should they be aware of the 'problems' that exist? When I said that 'people don't care', it's not that they're nasty, it's more that they're just blissfully unaware.

This all sounds very negative but let's not write off humanity just yet. I struggled at this particular point in my life and didn't know who to turn to for help or advice (amazingly, as you probably know already, support and literature for Aspergics (especially adults) is a little bit thin on the ground). The key is perseverance and making people understand. The trick though is not to sound like a martyr or as if you have some 'higher mission' (in other words, don't keep ramming it down people's throats).

Bridging the 'problem' gap

AS can be seen, in one respect, as a communication problem – and this is the area of AS that will affect employment more than any other. The problem with this is, how do you communicate that you have communication problem...when you have a communication problem? This is the challenge that faces both Aspergic employees (in that you can't explain your problems) and employers of Aspergic people (who need to find out what is wrong, recognize when things go (or are about to go) wrong and come up with the best strategy to avoid them and turn Mr/Mrs/Miss Aspergic into a happy (i.e. productive) worker).

I suppose that before looking at how to solve the communication problem, it might be a good idea to ask why we need to solve the communication problem at all. Given that it seems so difficult to make people understand (and that they may be reluctant to even *want* to understand), why bother? Why not just pretend that the problem doesn't exist and try to sweep it under the carpet? I've pondered this myself but if people are totally unaware of a problem then they have the ultimate defence if ever a problem *does* arise – 'Well I didn't know'. Also, why not try to raise people's perceptions? Why not try to educate them and help to see the world outside their safe little corner of it? It can also make life an awful lot easier for both you and 'them'. Trust me, if you try to ignore the issue then you quickly become a very depressed Aspergic bunny.

In my case I was very much aware of how other people around the company perceived me and there had been a couple of 'incidents' where my actions, reactions and responses had led to tension and problems. As part of my job I provide technical support for IT problems so often have to leave my little corner of comfort and journey out into the office, deal with the proletariat and, with a bit of luck, safely get back to my desk. No problem as I have a job to do and I can focus on that. The IT side of this particular task is easy (for me anyway) but life has transpired to throw all manner of spanners into even these simple tasks and it's the non-IT situations and elements that create problems and demonstrate why the need for greater understanding is blatantly obvious. Even getting to someone else's desk can be fraught with potential for disaster. It could be something as innocuous as passing someone in the corridor. What if they say something? What do I say back? What if there's a 'bump'? This might seem very innocent and 'ordinary' but for an Aspergic this is a nightmare situation. My response? Head down, ignore everyone and, with a bit of luck, I'll get where I need to get without any need for any of that human interaction stuff.

This kind of scenario (or rather the way to deal with this kind of scenario) is good for people like me in that it avoids confrontation and the need for interaction, but if you look at how this can come across to non-Aspergics then the impression that it leaves can be very negative. Aspergics can come across as being very cold, remote, arrogant, ignorant or even downright rude and uncaring. The truth is, we're not – we just don't live by the same rules when it comes to dealing with people. People may assume the worst when they only see the obvious and are unaware of the situation. A similar situation raises its head when the issue of 'small talk' comes up. If someone says to me 'lovely day' then I don't see that as the start of a conversation, I see that as a fact – it's merely a statement like 'buses are red' and 'the sky is blue'.

Often I've found that if people are aware of the situation then you can almost see the light bulb switching on above their heads – that moment of realization when you can see them thinking, 'Ah, so that explains…'. Explaining the situation and what it means is certainly not just to get these 'Ah' moments in other people but allows them to not only understand that sometimes you may come across as being 'weird' (and that it's not personal) but it also allows them to modify their approach and expecta-tions of you. There is also another effect and I certainly found that some people took the time to almost go out of their way to try. Not necessarily going overboard but just persevering with the 'good morning's and taking the trouble to say 'hello' as you passed them by. You could argue that it's the same situation as before, but once people are aware I found that the 'pres-sure' to respond was greatly reduced and I actually would respond since I knew that the chances of being drawn into a conversation about the weather (for example) were greatly reduced because people knew that it would make me uncomfortable. Also, by expressing an interest in you, people start to see past the ice cold exterior and realize that there is a human being inside. One person I'd worked with for nearly two years was astounded by the fact that not only could I string a sentence together but that I was actually a mine of useless information and seemed to know everything that there was to know about a certain time travelling doctor. By giving people that little nudge, metaphorically speaking, I found that most people got over their reservations and preconceptions and would actually make the effort, and they soon discovered that I actually *want* to talk to people, I just can't start conversations and I imagine that this is possibly the same with a lot of Aspergic people.

You might have noticed that in the last sentence of the last paragraph, I said '*most* people'. Yes, this is where we hit the big fat 'but'. Most people take the information onboard, process it and are fine with it – some make the effort and try to bridge the gap, others are aware and are just happy to let things carry on as normal. Then there are those people who just don't get it. I suppose I've been lucky in that this hasn't happened very often but some people have had negative responses. You can prepare yourself for this and, in my case, I simply adopted the basic attitude – 'If you have a problem with me being Aspergic…then *you* have a problem with me being Aspergic, not me'. Call that blasé if you like but people are generally afraid of things that they don't understand and Asperger Syndrome and autism in general are great mysteries to white-coated boffins, never mind Mr and Mrs Man-In-The-Street.

The need to adapt (both as an Aspergic employee and as an employer) is, I hope, very clear, but how can you go about raising awareness? Naturally, this will depend on the exact circumstances but I found that the worst thing to do was to try to explain everything or use medical jargon (you might have noticed that the terms 'neurotypical' and 'neuro-divergent' haven't cropped up in this article despite the fact that I think they're great). It's very easy to attempt to explain *everything* but this only leads to 'information overload' and most people simply switch off if you try it. This will sound clichéd but you really do need to keep it simple, and focus on only the aspects of Asperger's that will directly affect them – but make sure that they know that they can talk to you about it if they want to. You've lived with AS all of your life – they're starting afresh and are suddenly having to deal with something that, up until five seconds ago, they hadn't even heard of.

Now we reach the thorny issue how to actually get the message across. What about standing up and giving a big presentation explaining all about yourself and Asperger's? Already I can feel *myself* wanting to curl up in a little ball and just hide just at the thought of that approach. This just isn't going to work (the presentation bit, not the curling up in a ball bit – that always works) so what alternatives are there? Again, the exact circumstances may influence what media are available. My favourite is always email but this can often be interpreted as being a little bit impersonal. What about 'word of mouth'? Well you've got the problem of getting it started and then the worry about it turning into a game of Chinese Whispers. What worked for me was sitting down with one of the marketing people and going through what could be viewed as a mock interview. He'd ask questions (pre-arranged), I'd answer them and then *he'd* email them to everyone else. Why not just email them myself? The answer is simply that he asked the questions that 'normal' people would ask and not the questions that the Aspergic person *thinks* should be asked.

At the end of the day, though, it very much comes down to trial and error – you've got to keep trying until you find something that works for you.

How to help

I seem to have gone into great detail about why the 'communication gap' needs to be bridged, what's the best way to do it etc., but what happens if you're on the other side of the gap? How can employers and fellow employees help? As I keep saying, the problems encountered by one Aspergic may be totally different to those encountered by another so coming up with a set of hard-and-fast rules is nigh on impossible (key areas are communication and, although I haven't gone into it in this article, clear instructions, and trying to establish routines are also key points). The trick is to listen and show an interest and willingness to help (and actually helping of course, not just being *willing* to help). Some problems can't be fixed (for example, I have an aversion to working on days that have an 'a' in them) but usually a compromise or workaround can be found (in my case I get the weekend off each week). OK, so your Aspergic employee doesn't like going to team meetings – what about if they get the salient points of the meeting sent to them in an email? They still get the same information as everyone but don't have to be put through a nightmare situation. A simple workaround.

How a happy compromise and a happy work environment is achieved very much comes down to the individuals and the environment involved, and how willing everyone is to actually reach this mythical state of near nirvana. The lengths to which you may have to go naturally depend on the situation and circumstances but key to everything is listening and understanding, and even then there can be misunderstandings and 'issues'. I know that even though I've told the people that I work with time and time again that I have a communication problem, they still insist on saying 'Well, if you have a problem, just come and talk to me...' – I don't think they'll ever think this kind of statement through or realize what they're really saying (and if you are a non-Aspergic and have no idea what I'm going on about, how am I supposed to just 'come and talk to you' when I can't start a conversation?).

Conclusion

Working with Aspergic people can be very trying at times but it can also be very rewarding and Aspergics can bring a lot of skills and productivity to just about any workplace. Similarly, as an Aspergic trying to hold down a full-time job it can be very tough at times but it is definitely worth the effort.

As an Aspergic, when you make that decision to inform the workplace world it can be a very unsettling and worrying time (I often thought to myself 'Oh God, what have I done') but the vast majority of people will simply accept you just the way you are. Yes, your brain might be wired up differently but you're still the same person and most people, once they know about the situation, will be happy with that. Solving problems with AS in the workplace takes time but things do have a habit of sorting them-selves out...give it a couple of weeks and everybody (both Aspergic and non-Aspergic) will have forgotten what all the 'problems' were about.

Chapter 5: Case Study by an Employee with Asperger Syndrome and His Line Manager

Dean Worton and Paul Binks

Introduction by Luke Beardon

As Dean mentions – AS can be seen as a gift, and it pays to match the attributes of AS to a potential job. It can clearly be difficult explaining to a possible employer why having AS could contribute to a role, but certainly taking a positive outlook on the natural abilities AS offers an individual is a good way forward. People often note the honesty of individuals with AS, for example, or the time keeping, loyalty, precision, focus, dedication and so on. There is also the less-noted aspect, however, of the different ways of thinking that can be of high value indeed. I remember sitting in a meeting with Dean after having read something he had written and chatting to him about it. He had written that he doesn't often say much, but what he did say had a lot of thought behind it. I think this is the case for many people, and the insight some individuals have – as a result of having AS, not in spite of it – could be of immeasurable value to many employers.

The case study is divided into advice to individuals with Asperger Syndrome and employers, by Dean Worton, an individual with Asperger Syndrome, and tips for managers of people with Asperger Syndrome, by Dean's line manager Paul Binks, based on his experience.

Advice to individuals with Asperger Syndrome

In my adult life, I've had a wide variety of jobs and unpaid work placements with mixed success. Some have gone very well and at a few I didn't even survive the trial period. I was no stranger to being taken to one side with no prior hint of a problem and told that I was not up to the job and not given a chance to prove my worth over a longer trial period. In most cases, I thought I was doing well and getting on well with some of the staff until I found out all of a sudden that I was either not following the alleged correct social conventions by being too withdrawn and not considered 'part of the team' or because the speed I operated at was below the corporate quota. In one case it was because I kept making mistakes, yet no one actually sat down with me to see where I was going wrong. None of these jobs was high powered; they included a warehouse worker, hotel receptionist, check-out operator, data inputter and two office-based work placements. It seems that I just wasn't being given enough training. I do find it useful to have regular meetings with my manager, allowing us to get any problems out in the open and to look at solutions, as well as ongoing support from a mentor. This can also unearth successes as well as problems.

Some placements went well and I don't remember getting any negative reports from those, though on reflection they were probably fairly solitary-type jobs where I was left to work under my own initiative and complete tasks in my own way, thus allowing me to be creative. Those types of jobs are probably the best for me. They mainly involved filing, using databases or doing some other kind of computer-based project. My current job allows me to work in this way and is allowing me to really develop and be an asset to the organisation.

It was fortunate for me that my mother works with people with autistic spectrum disorders. What she explained to me about Asperger Syndrome made perfect sense and it was clear that the problems which I had been experiencing were all down to some sort of imbalance in my brain which was making me do things in a different way to most people. She told me about some of the work successes that people with Asperger Syndrome have had through either channelling their skills in the right area or receiving intensive training and/or mentoring when starting work, which enables them to do their job really well and shine.

I went forward with a more positive attitude. This was when I discovered the voluntary sector. I was introduced to the manager of a charity for people with severe learning disabilities. Eventually I was running the office on my own two days a week. I was in a building surrounded by other charities and integrated with their staff, including going on nights out. This gave me a great sense of confidence and I carried out the majority of administrative tasks as it was only a small charity and this gave me a great sense of worthiness and gave my life a purpose.

I was given the task of arranging an evening at the theatre for the charity's clients, which involved ringing the theatre. At that time, I found making important telephone calls to organizations a difficult thing to do, but in the end I had no other option but to do just that. After the charity folded due to lack of funding, I volunteered on a daily basis for a charity that used the same building. My main task was to set up a database of community meeting venues containing various pieces of detail such as cost, capacity, ward etc. I was required to make telephone calls in order to obtain some of the information. After this, not only had my database experience developed without my really noticing it but my telephone nerves were gradually diminishing. All this I was able to enter on my curriculum vitae and application forms. You are not obliged to state that the work was voluntary. Under job title, why put Volunteer when you could put Administration Assistant, Sales Assistant etc? This is not being dishonest. The employer will be more concerned with the tasks than 'splitting hairs' over whether you got paid for doing it. Experience counts more than what you actually got paid.

In the absence of paid work, the experience you gain from voluntary work will look great on your curriculum vitae and application form and by using positive language, it is possible to make a small task look really impressive. Even making tea and biscuits for visitors, could be described as 'responsible for providing hospitality to visitors from key partner organizations and ensuring their comfort and needs were adequately met'. You may think that such a description is a gross over-exaggeration, but in actual fact it is exactly what you were doing, its just that in a social situation, you probably wouldn't dream of explaining it like that, yet when applying for a job, it really is worth explaining everything using this sort of positive language. For more help with this try typing 'Positive Language' into a good search engine on the internet.

Starting my full-time voluntary placement coincided with joining a supported employment scheme. To find out about these look on the National Autistic Society's website www.nas.org.uk (accessed 15 January 2008) or type in 'Supported Employment' 'Asperger's' into a good search engine. You could use a combination of using and not using the apostrophe and adding or omitting the word 'Syndrome' as new results might come up every time. Not everyone will be so lucky but, within months, I had a full-time paid job. This was as the languages support officer of a small translation company. This allowed me to use my French, which I had had very little opportunity to use since completing my European languages and business degree. In this job, my use of databases was also put to good use and I had to answer the telephone a few times a day. Not only did this help me to overcome my telephone nerves, but I had a very professional yet caring telephone manner which I have carried over into my current job.

Even non-work activities can aid success in job interviews. In my spare time, I run a website for people with Asperger Syndrome in the UK entitled Aspie Village and host regular meet-ups for its members. When I was interviewed for my current job, I mentioned this and clearly impressed the panel and, throughout my job, my manager has often mentioned how much he has faith that I can do my job as well as I run my website. My job is an administration support role. This not only involves providing support to my department but also support to other departments throughout my organization. Senior managers ring me up for advice and reassurance and I am able to provide this through using similar skills to those I use on the website.

I have been in my current job for over a year. When applying for the role, again I received help from my support worker such as interview tips. I work for a large organization, which is very positive about disabilities. If the answers in the application form demonstrate that a disabled person meets all the essential criteria for the post, they are automatically offered an interview. Once in the interview situation, there is no further advantage, they are on an equal footing with anyone who is not disabled, but the great thing about this is that, while once in the interview the disabled person has no advantage over the non-disabled applicant, the non-disabled applicant also has no advantage.

In organizations with a 'Positive about Disabled People' logo (or similar if not in the UK), you generally gain points purely from the answers you give and not from how you came across. If one of the criteria in the person specification is to have 'good interpersonal skills' there is likely to be a question around this, so if you don't always come across well and cannot make eye contact, think, for example, of a situation where you dealt well with a customer and they went away feeling better and use the positive language mentioned above. Don't underestimate the worthiness of your answer. You might still gain maximum points for that question, even if you were making no eye contact when you tell them the story. However, you should at least attempt to make eye contact. Personally, I make unbroken eye contact when listening to the interviewer and the only time it sometimes falters is when answering a question because the gaze of the panel can at times make it extremely hard for me to think of my answer.

Although the scores are given for your answer and not for how you came across when giving your answer, this is not an exact science, so if you cannot guarantee reasonable eye contact, it may be useful to disclose your Asperger Syndrome before the interview commences. This is not shameful and having Asperger Syndrome is not shameful. I always say that I'm just telling them this in case they notice anything unusual during the interview, but also that they possibly won't. This way, the employer will probably mark you as highly as a non-disabled applicant. And remember, Asperger's is a gift and your unique thinking style will be sought after by employers, so don't miss out on this opportunity to shine. You could go through any entire interview situation in the public sector without making eye contact and still get the job, though its recommended to make some.

Of course, you might not have the same advantages if you are applying to an organization that does not have an equal opportunities policy, and in such a situation reasonable eye contact would probably be a prerequisite unless the employer sees something else in you that they like. Always make the best out of any job application situation and always think of the positive things that you have done and do not go into the interview thinking that they won't want to employ you because you haven't got a good track record in employment. You need to cast all those negative experiences aside. A good employer will not try to catch you out, and it would help to think of a creative answer if you are asked what your weaknesses are. For years, my stock answer in case I am ever asked this question is that at times I can get too enthusiastic and that maybe I don't always switch off from the job when I get home.

The public sector is where I have landed on my feet. I'm actually on a temporary contract at present but the likelihood is that I will be in a permanent position with my employer by the time this book is published. This does involve repeating the same application process I went through to gain my current job and being interviewed again, but in my organization there is an ethos of people being nurtured to work in a way best suited to them and I work in the department which exists to facilitate this. About a month into the job, I was getting a bit confused with part of my work and kept on making mistakes. I mentioned this to my manager and the situation was quickly resolved. Every other month during our trial period we have probationary reviews. At first, this was an unsettling idea. I did admit at these that I had struggled with one particular project. However, my manager didn't react with the usual 'Must do Better' answer, but used the organization's training ethos of 'There is no failure, only development'. I collect quarterly and annual data from senior managers and sometimes this requires an assertive nature. A few years ago, I could go to a party not knowing anyone and sit there for two hours not speaking until finally spoken to, and I usually wait to be spoken to if passing a colleague on the corridor, but I have developed the confidence to ring managers with late data and tell them how important it is that they submit it. I also write reports and produce spreadsheets and other filing systems, which makes the administration of data much more simple and informative. Not only am I developing but my ideas contribute towards the development of the department which may also benefit the organization and its delivery to members of the public from all walks of life.

I would recommend any Aspie to look for work in the public sector. It is very difficult to lose your job in the public sector and unlike in the private sector you would probably have to do something illegal to be instantly dismissed. If you are unlucky enough for your performance to lead to disciplinary procedures, you would have ample opportunity to solve the problems and potentially become a model employee and stay in the job for life. I truly believe that Aspies usually just need a chance to prove themselves.

All too often, an Aspie can look good on paper and then not match this at the interview because sadly personality seems to matter so much more in this scenario and this can be where Aspies can become victims of the 'I can work someone out within thirty seconds of meeting them' attitude. We've all seen movies that seemed unpromising for the first ten minutes, but turned out to be one of the most inspired movies we've ever seen. I think Aspies need employers who are willing to take time to watch the whole movie about them and not dismiss them at interview because the commercial was bland or in the first few days of employment because they don't seem to be picking the job up. Any movie can be good with a good producer, so in my opinion a good employer can create a good Asperger employee.

Public sector organizations – councils, hospitals, universities, etc. – usually only look at people's answers in interviews. They are only interested in the words, and not in penalizing you for how you say them. You need to read the Person Specification and Job Description. In the Person Specification, think about how you can meet the essential criteria. You can often meet these better than you think. Even if you've done something just once, it counts and it doesn't necessarily have to have even been in a work situation. For example, if they are asking for a confident telephone manner, but you have never used the telephone at work, maybe you can relate this to ringing an organization from home. You could even ring potential employers to get this experience and gain confidence on the telephone, as this is a transferable skill. You could feel very nervous in an interview and be convinced that you didn't get the job, and still get it anyway because while the panel may have noticed your nervousness, they were impressed with your answers and feel that you can do the job well.

Look for an employer who respects you and is interested in what you are able to offer and don't dismiss you offhand for some minor discrepancy. They do exist. So if you think you have skills and qualities to offer if someone will just allow you to, then there is an employer out there who is waiting for you to come along and will give you that chance. Just sell yourself at the interview and go along with the attitude that no one is a better person than you are. We are all equal and you deserve to be treated that way. If it's too soon to start a paid job, make yourself indispensable to a voluntary organization for free in the mean time.

Advice to employers of individuals with Asperger Syndrome

If you are a private sector employer, you should always give employees or applicants with Asperger Syndrome a reasonable chance. You should be asking 'Can they do the job?' not how well do they interact, unless the very nature of the job involves constant direct contact with people. With someone with Asperger Syndrome, the body language doesn't always give as true an impression as it does with someone without Asperger Syndrome. You should disregard body language, and rely only on what they tell you in an interview situation. If the job involves high-powered handling of clients and the Asperger traits make that unrealistic, the candidate is unlikely in any case to be able to give the answers that get them the job, but where the answers do get them a job, this should be trusted and not disbelieved as soon as the Aspie makes their first error or social gaffe. This is because Asperger Syndrome is a developmental disorder and it can take a bit longer to pick things up. It's the same analogy as taking twice as long to fill a shelf as you asked, but having perfect presentation. People with AS can be very through and their work is often slow because it is good quality when finally complete. Therefore not only is patience necessary but can also be very rewarding.

In the public sector, it is more difficult to dismiss an employee that you feel is not 'up to standard' but whether you are a public, private or voluntary sector employer then you need to be prepared to make 'reasonable adjustments' for the Asperger employee. Always make sure that they feel valued and always look for ways that they can reach their true potential. A good thing to do would be to set up an informal one-to-one meeting with them now and again and ask them if there are any tasks that they would particularly like to do. It may be that they can be useful in an area that someone doing their job maybe wouldn't normally do. Its very important that all of their capabilities are recognized. Many of the world's greatest minds were thought to have had Asperger Syndrome, but perfection would probably be impossible without making a few mistakes along the way.

Explain things slowly and gently while still treating them like an adult. Seek clarification every so often that they understand the explanation and encourage them to take notes if they wish and ask them if they have any questions so far. An employee with AS should also have a mentor that they can speak to as they will be more impartial. It may be useful to allow an unpaid trial before joining the pay roll.

You should also help the AS employee to integrate into the organization. People with AS are more likely to wait to be approached. Because employees tend not to expend much time on making new employees feel comfortable, the result can be that the other employees feel that the AS employee is not fitting in. However, with the right sort of intervention they may be able to fit in very easily. You should ask the AS employee who they wish to know that they have AS and advise them that it will make their life easier if their immediate colleagues are aware, so that anything that seems slightly unusual should be accepted and not made an issue of, and possibly not even mentioned.

My manager Paul Binks kindly offered to write his own advice based on his own experience of working with someone with Asperger Syndrome and his advice from a manager's point of view is included below as a complement to my own case study.

Employment case study: tips for working with some one with Asperger's and working if you have Asperger's
By Paul Binks, manager of individual with Asperger Syndrome
SHORTLISTING
Most organizations have a policy that anyone who is registered disabled and meets the essential criteria for the job specification will be included on the shortlist for interview. As a manager you will get a good first impression of a candidate if they present a good application form. Asperger's will probably not restrict someone filling out an application well, though they may have had more limited opportunities in employment to draw experiences on. As a candidate with Asperger's it is always worth the effort to submit the best application form you can. Make sure you look at the essential and desirable skills/abilities/knowledge and tailor your application to specifically addressing these rather than listing chronologically your experiences and abilities etc. If you don't get shortlisted ask for feedback on your applications.

INTERVIEWS
As a manager is it worth familiarizing yourself with information on Asperger's. Sometimes a person with Asperger's may display behaviour that you do not expect at an interview and, in a person without Asperger's, you may read this behaviour as making them unsuitable for the job. For example, some people with Asperger's will not make eye contact when thinking about their answer to questions and when responding. This is part of their disability and should not be 'held against them'. Most HR

departments will have only limited experience of dealing with people with Asperger's. Information about Asperger's should therefore be sought from other sources. The interview panel should carefully consider this information before the interview.

The skills, abilities and behavioural traits of people with Asperger's will mean that they may be more suitable for some types of jobs than others. People with Asperger's can be very good at certain roles that require appreciation to detail, for example. When being interviewed a person with Asperger's is on a 'level playing field' with other candidates. The post should always be awarded to the candidate who performs best on the day against the marking criteria set out in the job specification. When interviewed, a person with Asperger's may have limited work experience to draw on. It is worth asking them about any voluntary work they have done for relevant experience and not just relying on work experience.

As a person with Asperger's you will know your own limitations and the sort of situations you like to be in and ones that you don't. After the formal questioning interviewers will usually ask if you have any questions. Do not be afraid to ask questions. Most interviewers will be trained to only use your answers to the formal questions to make a judgement on your suitability for the post. They should not hold any questions you ask after the informal questions against you. Use the opportunity to ask questions about the job and what you will be doing. If you do not feel comfortable to ask questions in this situation you can always wait until you are offered the post to ask additional questions.

If you do not get offered the post it would be useful to ask for feedback on your performance, This is usually offered and given objectively. You can use the feedback to help prepare for other interviews. Don't be put off applying for other jobs if you are not successful. Getting a good job isn't easy whether you have a disability or not.

THE WORKPLACE
As a manager you are responsible for the well-being of all your employees. Under the Disability Discrimination Act 1995 all employers have to make reasonable adjustments to allow people with a disability to carry out their work. It is reasonably easy to correctly assume the sort of adjustments someone with a physical disability would need. However, you should never assume that you know best; consultation with the individual about their needs and what you can do to help them is essential. The same applies

for someone with Asperger's, though it is even more important to consult with them as the adjustments aren't always immediately apparent. It is important as a manager to have an overall appreciation of Asperger's, to discuss with the employee how best to help them but also to review the way the two of you are working and be prepared to change things. People with Asperger's can be very good at certain types of work, particularly where attention to detail is required. Getting the best results from them can take a bit of patience but is worth the effort. The sort of adjustments that will be required will be particular to the individual. Some of the things that could be trialled are:

- giving the individual time to make their own notes when being instructed to do a task
- letting them work out the best way to do something for themselves
- giving them clear instructions written down or a template to follow
- giving them the time to work things out but arranging a definite time when you will check back with them
- providing them with a clear time frame of when things need to be done by.

Always be patient, offer positive feedback and work with the individual to identify how else they can do something if your previous approach hasn't worked.

Regardless of how you prepare for someone with Asperger's your appreciation of the individual and their disability will grow over time. Be prepared to accept the disability and work with the individual's strengths and weaknesses.

At the outset of employment, ask the individual if you can share with their immediate team the fact that they have Asperger's; they may not want you to do this and you must respect their wishes. It is an advantage, though, for the immediate team members to have an appreciation of Asperger's so that they can support the individual. It may also help the individual to settle in better. There are a number of organizations that can offer bespoke training or you can do it more discreetly yourself in a team meeting for instance. As part of the Asperger's an individual may show certain types of behaviour: not making eye contact, not liking sudden loud noises, not liking to be in a reasonably small space with others (such as lifts or kitchen areas), not finding it easy to say 'Hello' to people they have not formally met, for instance. People within the office may notice this behaviour. It is human nature that they will question it and wonder why the person is like that. A person with Asperger's may come across as being ignorant if other people do not understand what Asperger's as a disability is. As a manager it is important to keep an eye on how these interactions are taking place. Discuss them with the employee that has Asperger's. It might be worth mentioning to them that if other people knew about Asperger's then they would understand why the employee is as they are and the employee might feel more integrated. In the end the decision is that of the employee. If other employees make comments or remarks about the person with Asperger's then as a manager you must support the individual with Asperger's; in extreme cases this may mean taking disciplinary action against others who make fun of their behaviour, for example. Hopefully, though, with careful management situations like this will not arise.

Other support that can be provided may be in the form of a mentor, possibly from the HR section. There are also organizations that can provide support. These can be useful to help the individual talk about work problems and even try and manage aspects of their Asperger's that they would like to change. Consider giving the employee some time on a regular basis to meet with their mentor.

As a person with Asperger's you may feel daunted on your first day at work. This is natural; everyone feels like this. Just remember that you got the job on your own merits and your employers chose you above others as they had faith in you and your ability to do the job. Your first few days or weeks will usually be quite structured as you get used to the job and being in the work environment. Take this opportunity to get to know the work but also the people around you. If you have any concerns make sure you talk to your manager about them.

Carefully consider whether you want people to know about your Asperger's. If your immediate work colleagues know and understand about Asperger's they may more easily be able to help you out and this may help you settle in more easily. If you make a decision to only let a small number of people know then after a month or so discuss with your manager whether it would be appropriate to let other people know. In the end it is your decision but it might help you to integrate into the workplace more.

Take the opportunity to have a workplace or other mentor. Mentors can be useful in helping you by listening to any concerns you have, offering advice and providing help with practical things that might be bothering you either in work or in your private life. They may also be able to act as an advocate for you if you don't feel confident in approaching your manager or others.

Generally speaking, remember that any work situation is strange to begin with. You may not immediately feel at home in your surroundings or with the work. If you don't feel at ease or if you are unsure about any aspect of your work do not be afraid to speak to your manager. Managers will be busy and may not immediately be able to see you but if this is the case arrange a specific time when you can sit down together. In fact, when you first start it might be worth diarying a couple of meetings in advance. It is your manager's job to listen to any concerns you have and to address any problems you may encounter.

Chapter 6: The World of Work (Is Not on Another Planet) and my Journey to Getting There

Dr John Biddulph

Introduction by Luke Beardon

There could be much to comment on in this chapter – the wonderful dry sense of humour, the insight, the openness – but one thing more than anything stands out for me: the last sentence. A superb summing-up statement presented by a highly intelligent individual. The very notion that it is the person with AS who has to make significant adjustments is abhorrent. We live in a society with actual laws to protect against discrimination in the workplace, and yet we still have so many individuals who have to make adjustments themselves in order to 'fit in'. Why is it that it should be down to the individual with AS to make all the changes? Why should someone like John, who has an incredible brain and should be a treasured member of staff, have to behave in ways that are unnatural and stressful? There are obvious answers, but in simple terms I think that ignorance is at the heart of the matter – and in this case, ignorance is, most definitely, not bliss.

Dilemma: Fishing or A-level chemistry revision.

Outcome: Three sizeable rainbow trout and 'grades not quite meeting our expectations'.

I am 18 years and 1 month old. I am studying for four A-levels and have good offers to read chemistry at two redbrick universities with good reputations. The future is bright. The future is…teatime. The float plops onto the River Derwent and the current and lead shot combine to cause the float to trot gently downstream.

Full of fish and admiration for my own fishing skills, I reach for my salmon-pink chemistry exercise book. There are gaps. Blank pages full of failed experiments. I reach for my comfort object; my memory. It has served me well so far. Even at times when I didn't think I knew something, my memory would serve it up obligingly on a plate of delights. The blank pages? Well, I discovered Marcel Proust at the same time as my greatest scientific discovery. Mrs Bradbury (the chemistry lab assistant) would leave the bottles of chemicals used in constructing the compound for us to analyse on her bench. Two hours of testing for different substances – or works of great literature under my bench? No contest. I was always grateful to Mrs Bradbury for her support. Like the day when I found her moving a jar of old sodium to the chemical store for disposal later. I wondered what a quantity of sodium would look like when exposed to water. I knew the answer already and I liked questions like that. Why do teachers ask questions that they know the answer to and most or even all of the class don't – teachers call it diagnostic but I call it stupid and I did occasionally though not always to my advantage. Helpfully, I suggested to Mrs Bradbury that Mr Davenport (deputy head teacher and head of chemistry) would dispose of it down the nearest drain to save time and to save the naptha that the sodium is swimming in. Anyone would know that you don't put sodium (especially a piece the size of a half house-brick) in water so the lab assistant surely wouldn't do it. Outcome: two drain covers rocket past the top of the sports hall, a small, but perfectly formed fireball whistles past Mrs Bradbury's nose and I have some explaining to do. This is pointless. Everybody knows what happens when you add sodium to water.

Dilemma: Science or the Arts?

Outcome: I wake up one morning and decide to go to music college instead of studying chemistry.

It was not a gradual process, an emerging idea or even an epiphany. It happened in an instant, in the twinkling of an eye. (The next career-changing instant happens almost 30 years later but was no less dramatic.) 'So you want to be a musician?' asks the person in charge of grants at the County Offices. 'Yes', I reply. 'When did you decide; it's a big step?' 'This morning.' Things go quiet for a while and then, after some encouragement, I offer what must have been a plausible explanation and I am offered a three-year grant. Two auditions later and I am enrolled on a three-year course to study music and electronic music composition.

Day-to-day life at music college is a strange experience. I am expected to stay in a room and practise for hours a day. This seems OK. I meet a good friend Dave who is an architect and excellent musician and we form a band. A school friend happens to be studying architecture too at the same place and he has a flat with his wife (I composed the music for their wedding). He offers me accommodation in year two and I have a sleeping bag and a mattress as well as my music textbooks and instruments. Weekends see me back home with my dad. I have my first job teaching clarinet and saxophone in my old school on Fridays. Mrs Rowlands, my old English teacher, who hit me on the head with the Complete Works of Shakespeare, is strangely different with me now. Perhaps she realizes now that my fascination with the tree on the other side of the playground was a means of concentrating, a focusing activity, not an act of defiance. 'Biddulph, what were the last words Caesar spoke to Brutus?' she intones across room 2 as the tree occupies my gaze. 'Et tu, Brute?' Biddulph turns his head and responds. She erupts. Why? I gave the correct answer.

> Milestones: I get through year one at music college and progress to year two despite poor attendance. I have engaged substantially with some elements: electronic composition has gone very well.

My clarinet playing has not progressed as well as expected. I intend to put this right in year two by getting a couple of diplomas. Year two and I get a couple of diplomas on the clarinet and manage to have steak pie, chips and peas and a black cherry yoghurt for every evening meal whilst attending college. That's almost 120 steak pies and 120 yoghurts, a lot of chips; I didn't count the peas. Year three: I am asked by my piano teacher

Mrs Horner if I am mentally ill[1] and I graduate and get a place to do a Post-graduate Certificate in Education in Birmingham. I have fallen into the education funnel after giving myself a considerable amount of careers advice just before leaving music college in the form of a simple question: What am I going to do next?

I go to Birmingham with a cocktail of anxiety and excitement. I meet my life partner there on the same course as I am on and on the first day. The ice-breaker challenge is to talk to somebody you don't know. I remain motionless. I am approached in a crowded room by the very image of female perfection. A brief conversation is initiated – not by me. 'I went to music college there, did you like it?' I enter the conversation with my usual aplomb: 'No,' I reply and walk off to another quieter part of the room. I wonder if my opening gambit in developing a friendship with this person (now my wife of some 24 years) will work. It did! Our friendship develops after what I later discover was a slightly rocky start and my wife-to-be (who wears glasses) recognizes me by my walk. I have (at this time in my life) a pronounced spring in my step at all times.

> Dilemma: What should I play at my interview for the post of instru-mental music teacher?

> Outcome: I get the date of the interview wrong and end up standing at the bus stop in my suit with my clarinet case just seven days too late. The post has been filled.

Getting the date of the interview wrong for my first teaching post inter-view was a bit of a shock to the system. I resolve to get it right next time and am lucky enough to be offered another interview only three weeks later in a nearby local education authority.

I turn up and I am the only one for interview. Good, I still like being on my own a lot. I leave two hours later with my first job offer under my belt and a feeling of relief that my mistake over the date of the previous inter-view hasn't proven too costly.

---

1   I have the capacity to memorize large amounts of music. I can also busk well but can't get the technique exactly right so I tend to learn the basics of a piano piece and make the rest up, resulting in a (usually) passable version of the original – my piano teacher didn't share my view.

I am in gainful employment for the first time in my life. I visit schools teaching children to play woodwind instruments, play the saxophone in the authority big band (which I later direct for eight years) and conduct and direct other music ensembles as well as getting to practise the clarinet and sax a lot if a pupil does not turn up for their lesson in a small room in one of several schools. I am peripatetic. I am in charge of who I teach and there is little in the way of staff meetings, parents' evening etc. Perfect! For now.

The profession is littered with oddballs, except me of course. A colleague moves from a flat in Birmingham to a more local flat some 17 miles away. He walks back and forth all weekend carrying his belongings in dustbin liners.

I decide to write a six-page suggestion in the suggestions book in the staff room. It is torn out and I haven't the inclination to write it in again. That will teach me to have grand ideas about restructuring the musical ensembles and staffing only nine months into my first post. I never asked what happened to it.

> Milestones: I develop my interest in electronic composition more and
> run some workshops in same.

After three years, and with a slight tinge of regret, I move to work for a bigger education authority that will give me car loan as well as better prospects. I acquire a beige Renault 4 but I later discover the promise of better prospects to be untrue. The second post is much the same as the first. I am beginning to get very bored with teaching people to play woodwind instruments. However, I do toe the line and when a school is closed I duly turn up at the central office as I am supposed to do. The phone rings so I look around in the hope that someone else will answer it. No one is around so I pick up the phone. I announce my name and the service I work for. The person asks me what I do so I tell them. I teach people to play woodwind instruments. The caller then develops a more pompous tone and demands to speak to my superior. I tell the caller that no one is my superior and put the telephone receiver down. There is no comeback. This is not a surprise as I was not expecting one. I get the impression that I annoy some of my colleagues because they treat me in ways that even I can see are unkind. To this day, I have absolutely no idea why.

Whilst working in this authority I run courses in composition and electronic music for my 'old' authority and develop a real interest in music from different cultures. I get my first commission as a composer.

> Dilemma: Do I remain an instrumental teacher or do I try to find something else?

> Outcome: I enrage my current employers and my head of service in particular by applying for a senior post in a school. I enrage them still further by performing so well in the interview that I am offered and accept the position.

I go from an assistant teacher pay scale to a senior teacher pay scale. Outside of work I really start to develop a very strong interest in computers and teach myself how to programme. Not for the first time in my life, I talk about my interests and bore someone to tears, but this time it is literally that. Our visitor listens to me for a while (two hours) and then bursts into tears. There is nothing about the information concerning the life and music of Frederick Delius that could cause offence or extreme sadness so I can only assume that the duration and intensity of the discourse were responsible.

I am a head of department! I work in a large comprehensive school in an inner city multi-ethnic area. It is wonderful. I am in control of my own domain, running the department, commenting on and developing school policy and practice, and making music with young people. I can run choirs, electronic music groups, run workshops, organize arts weeks, have visits from advisors and colleagues who have been told that I am good at my job and do an MA in arts education by research. My Asian music group win the National Festival of Music for Youth and appear at the Albert Hall and on a few BBC programmes about music in schools. They get a recording deal and I play as a session musician on more than one album. The week after the third album's release, I am on a recording that is No. 1 in the UK Bhangra Charts. I call a choir practice (the choir is 100 strong) and someone triggers a fire alarm drill. 'Do I have a list?' 'No.' I am asked how anyone will know where the pupils are. I still struggle with some issues. I later learn that the drill was for my benefit to teach me a lesson. If the deputy head responsible had explained to me that a register was required I would have done it and it would have saved almost 1000 children and 50 teachers lining up on the playground. Minor incidents like this apart (there were a few others) I have the most wonderful time working in this school. My colleagues seem to understand me most of the time and working with the children doing music is about as good as it gets.

Does it get much better? For eight years the answer is no and then I make a fundamental error. I absorb the education profession's malaise of looking for furtherment. Fortunately, I am unsuccessful in my two attempts to become an Local Education Authority (LEA) inspector (music) although I manage to get through to the final round of the selection process on both occasions. I am told my experience is limited. How can they know, they only interviewed me for about one hour. The interview process is strange but I really enjoy it. The part I find very difficult is when they take you for lunch, show you round a primary school, introduce you to prospective colleagues and try to reassure you with the 'this is not part of the selection process' lie. It clearly is and it is probably my weakest area. Despite the fact that I know it is a lie, I still can't get myself sufficiently into pretend mode and I imagine that the conclusion drawn is that I am not good at talking to people. This is ridiculous because I am very good at talking to people in the workplace. I know a lot about my subject, know a lot about what other people think and write about my subject and have a lot of experience of talking to people in the workplace.

The way they chose to determine this in interviews is ridiculous and unfair.

However, the interview process is about to play a trick on me and it turns out that the trick is not a particularly amusing one.

Remember the place I mentioned earlier that I attended as a postgraduate student to learn how to teach? I apply for a post there and get it. I leave the secondary school tinged with regret but also pleased I have accessed higher education. I am a Senior Lecturer in Music Education, Director of a Music Technology Studio and (although I didn't know it at the time of the interview) a Course Director.

I start my job in the faculty of education. A few days into the job and I am invited (not for the only time) to see the Dean of the faculty, who asks me how long it will take to relieve myself of the directorship of the youth jazz orchestra I conduct on an evening. Apart from a little (internal) giggle about 'relieving myself', I am completely baffled by the request. I go back and share my confusion with my two colleagues. They explain to me that I am to be running a course on Thursday evenings for serving teachers and that I will need to resign my jazz orchestra post. I am even more confused.

How did they know this was the case? How did they know that I was to be course director (especially when one of them was already doing this job) and how come, when my musicianly activities were celebrated at my interview, I am being asked to give up the one I like doing the most only one week in to my new job? I feel betrayed and indignant that the interview process did not reveal all of the opportunities coming my way.

The way the job develops is frustrating. I really like the opportunity to work alone, to research (in small quantities – yet the irony is that my employers expect large quantities because it directly affects funding). I also like working with students but the amount of administration, bureaucracy and unkindness is extraordinary.

I am a year and a bit into my job at the university. I am invited to see the Dean of the faculty for a second time. I am not a good team player. I tell the Dean that there is always more than one player in a team and the best teams work together as a unit complementing rather than duplicating skills. Not for the first time, I suspect my response is not quite what he expected. My colleagues are very different to me. They waste time telling each other what they are doing and how well they are doing it. I waste time learning how to programme computers and compose music. As far as I am concerned, my time-wasting is preferable to theirs.

Next delight: I am made a course director for the second time. This time my course is run jointly by my own faculty and the faculty of music. I find myself in good company as my colleagues in the music faculty seem to like me well enough. They seem far more inclined to celebrate my strengths and support my deficits. Good enough. For a while longer.

A post becomes vacant in the faculty which I am not supposed to apply for. My other colleague is, I understand from some of my friends in the music faculty, 'destined' for the position. This destiny strikes me as unfair and I request an application form and details from the faculty office because I am much better at the important things than her. I fill in the form and hand it to the Dean of the faculty. He seems surprised. A few days later he tells me I have constructed a very good application. This means I am not going to get the job. At this stage in my life, I have started to 'read between the lines'. I get an interview to add to the farcical nature of the process. I do a storming interview (which was my plan) and then wait. My office telephone rings. No one speaks and I recognize the voice talking in the background, the second interviewer. The phone is immediately slammed down. The Dean has rung me by mistake. He intended to ring my colleague to convey the good news.

Minutes later, I get a call from the same number asking me to attend the Dean's office. I then get the usual 15 minutes of total nonsense known euphemistically as a 'debriefing' where the interview panel avoid telling you why you haven't got the job because if they did, you would be able to take legal action against them. Debriefing is almost as stupid as going fishing the day before an A-level examination. It gives you absolutely no idea as to why you haven't been successful in that application and interview process and even less of an idea of how you might 'improve' to do better in the next one unless, of course, the interviewers know exactly what post you are going to apply for, what the job description is and what questions you will be asked at the next interview. The trouble is, many people on interview panels pretend that this is precisely what they know and ask ridiculous questions like 'What do you think about equal opportunities?'

On the up side, many colleagues in the faculty tell me (quietly) that they would have rather seen me in the director of school post and this makes me feel, well, nothing to be honest. I only applied because I knew that I could do the job.

My colleague suddenly is my manager. I have an Internal Performance Review (IPR) meeting and this lasts more than the official time, more than half a day in fact and I manage to describe how I feel in post in a little detail; not as much as I would have liked as I am very frustrated by the opportunities I get at work – none. I know that I am not entitled to opportunities but I will do better if I am provided with some. I know this because I read it in a book and to some extent it is true. The full extent of the truth though is that I need be involved in the selection of these opportunities. At the end of the interview I am asked if I feel that I am a fish out of water. I know what this means and I know some of the implications so I consider my answer quite carefully. No, I respond, I often feel like a fish in sewerage and sometimes very thick sewerage at that.

I leave the IPR feeling it best to have said this as it really does convey how I feel sometimes and I have had problems expressing this, so clearly it is a step forward.

The level of persecution increases inversely proportionate to my opportunities which are ground zero. The fact that my ratings from students in evaluations still seem to rate me quite highly seems to make the situation worse. How can this be? The students seem to rate my work as 'good' and, as luck would have it, we undergo an HMI inspection a few weeks later where my sessions are given top marks as well as my development of online resources. I can only describe my colleagues' reaction to this as 'frosty' even though it's not a word I would use to describe reactions normally.

One day, I go in to work with a really bad cold and a voice worthy of any Russian bass-baritone. The next day I have pneumonia. I have hardly ever had time off work for illness in 20 years. The doctor signs me off work for some considerable time. I have plenty of time for thinking and writing references which my colleagues thoughtfully send me by email. I also get phone calls from the course administrator on a regular basis.

After being ill for two months I wake up one day to find my wife on the phone to her brother. 'Tell him I'm not going back to work at the university any more.' I remark as I struggle to the cupboard for my antibiotics. When the phone call ends she looks slightly puzzled. We have not discussed this or the impact it will have on our lives (we have three children now).

I tell her that I have decided to pursue my skills as a computer programmer and write databases for internet-based technologies. I have taught myself to do this and it is reasonably easy. I predict that many companies will need this service as it is relatively early days in terms of the internet and technologies are only just emerging.

I can also work from home.

When I return to collect my belongings from the faculty after being ill for five months one colleague avoids me, another makes a sarcastic comment and everyone else is really kind and thoughtful. Apparently during my prolonged absence, my office computer has been scrutinized for any 'incriminating' evidence. Evidence of what? My intelligence, my success? No, I suspect not. I think it was examined to see if there were any documents offering evidence that I did work outside of the faculty: courses, conferences and the like. How do I know this? Someone in the faculty tells me just before I leave.

My world of work has changed dramatically. I have a company. I am a business man! I am a secretary. I am finance person. I am the tea maker. I am the sole provider of services to clients. I do the VAT returns. I answer the telephone. I buy the paper for the printer. I have to access new clients and build the business. Before doing this I have to get my first real client. My

ASPERGER SYNDROME AND EMPLOYMENT

company website is attracting attention and I get one or two unsolicited enquires. Email contact is great. Talking to prospective clients on the phone is not my strong suite. However, a few weeks pass and things start to happen.

I get an email from a company in London. It is a big company, a very big company, and I provide them with a proposal. I am quite good at writing proposals and to my delight I receive an email inviting me to their offices in Lincoln's Inn Fields. I know this to be the old place of executions (I hope not my own) and location of the Royal College of Surgeons.

I arrive in the Lincoln's Inn with my laptop and a degree of optimism. I enjoy making presentations and the draft Chinese version of the website and database has worked out well. I have even learned a small amount of Mandarin to introduce the presentation. I read the sign outside the very large office building and walk in. Something strikes me about the sign but I can't work out what it is. I tell them who I am at reception and I am ushered upstairs into a waiting room. I am in the waiting room with about ten other people. This strikes me as a little odd as I was told that only three companies were 'pitching' for the job. Pitching – I had never heard this word before as I was totally new to this world of work.

I listen but say little to my competition. It emerges that one set of competitors is from the largest telecoms group in the UK and the other is a company from Bristol with a multi-million pound turnover. As yet, I am a company of one with no turnover whatsoever. Each company has sent a team of five people to 'pitch' for the job. I wait my turn. When I eventually enter the room I am greeted by a panel of 15 people.

I suddenly realize that the sign outside conveyed a very important message – the correct name of the company. In my presentation I have two words in the wrong order. I ask for a few moments to prepare. During this time I open my presentation and do a search and replace, correcting all the incorrect references to the company name. This done, I turn round and announce that I am ready to start.

I make my presentation (the Mandarin seems to go down well) and I make them laugh with a few improvised remarks. I will be contacted the next day by telephone. I leave to catch the train home feeling satisfied with my performance but not overly optimistic.

The next day the phone rings. I have won the contract to build and supply the online services for this company – six months' work for me. It turns out to be a nightmare as my experience of working with a big company is non-existent and I make a lot of mistakes in terms of securing staged payments for my work (I earn virtually nothing for this period) and agreements in terms of exactly what I will provide, so I find myself producing more and more work and everything seems to need revisions even though I think I have supplied exactly what they ask for.

Another stroke of good fortune befalls me. An ex-colleague from the university (though not the same department) who has moved on to work for another organization contacts me. One of my friends from the university (a colleague from yet another department) has told of my diversification into internet-based technologies. I am asked if I would consider working for a special needs education organization as their supplier of internet-based technologies. This sounds wonderful and I respond very positively. It's in my newly acquired career specialism; it's connected to my previous specialism (education) and it's in an area that I am very interested in: special needs. It doesn't get much better does it?

There is a catch. I have to go abroad for an interview. What? I am 44 years old and I have never set foot on an aircraft in my life.

I turn up at Birmingham airport accompanied by my prospective new colleague. I am exhausted. I have slept no more than five minutes the previous night. No, that's an exaggeration. I have slept no more than three minutes the previous night and I am consumed with anxiety.

I go through the preliminaries and I walk nervously to the gate. I board the aircraft. My pulse is not just racing, it's almost blurred into one. The aircraft engines are started. Surely there's something wrong. This is a sophisticated mode of travel. How can efficient jet engines (that are working properly) be this loud? It is early in the morning and the aircraft begins to taxi down the runway. My hands are white as they clench the arm rests. As the aircraft turns and the engines roar into an acceleration frenzy, I feel like I am going to explode, which is curious because that's precisely what I feel the aircraft is going to do. It lifts into the air followed in varying degrees by my internal organs, then everything seems to catch up and relocate in a strange rearrangement in my body, I see the ground disappearing fast beneath me. The only problem is that between me and the ground several thousand feet below is a steel tube being propelled forwards by its shape and some exploding kerosene that gives rise, through a worryingly simple device, to propulsion. I have no idea if the little dips and bumps are significant but they are really worrying (my travelling companion tells me that this is called 'turbulence' – I know and understand what turbulence is and this is the cause not the effect – I like it best when people describe the effect as well). The descent is no better than the take-off and the bit in between was momentarily interrupted by a stale bread bun with a piece of cheese that would not have tempted a mouse ravaged by weeks of starvation.

Two hideous hours later and we hit the tarmac. I am equally alarmed by the brutality of the landing, which causes me to wonder if I am doing the right thing. Worse still, I have the return journey to come. Somewhere in Europe now is a Boeing 737-200 that has aisle seat 15 with armrests that have indentations that will accommodate my hand shapes to perfection.

By comparison, the train ride to the middle of the country is very enjoyable, although it is tainted by my slow recovery from my first flight and my total fatigue.

I arrive at the offices of the organization I might work for. In fact, after a very pleasant talk to the director, I discover that he has made a decision already, based on my application, speaking to me on the phone and from talking to my ex-colleague from the university who now works for this organization. I have a new part-time job.

The journey back is equally horrible. Why doesn't somebody give a commentary on planes? That bump was all right. That noise is perfectly normal. This is how this particular aircraft taxis under entirely normal circumstances. This amount of thrust is enough to get us into the air and keep us there. The noise from the retracting parts at the rear of the wings is what is expected and they are used only for take-off and landing to provide additional lift. Why doesn't somebody do this? It just seems to make sense to me.

I start my work redesigning the internet elements of the organization's information dissemination system and all seems well for the time being. Working from home seems agreeable enough. The 'growing the business' part of being a company does not come to me in a very natural way and I think I might struggle to develop things in the future. For now, though, I have a part-time job with an organization that seems to have time for me as well as my skills and sufficient additional work with a small number of companies that will keep things going for a while.

A meeting: five days and in a Scandinavian country. Sounds exciting but fills me with fear. Worse is to come when I discover it is two flights there and two flights back. Being in Scandinavia is enjoyable and I get to taste reindeer on a small boat on the Baltic Sea. We meet in the world trade centre where I access the network to enable us to use their internet connection after no one is available to permit us legitimate use. My colleagues seem impressed by my skills on the computer and are very positive about a joint presentation I give on internet information dissemination at the end of the five-day meeting.

Things are going well.

> Dilemma: I can't work out if I'm earning enough money or not and whether or not money in the company account is available for everyday use.

> Outcome: I don't pay myself any salary for the first year in order to make sure I have enough to pay things like Corporation Tax, VAT and the like.

> Additional outcome: As I have accumulated a reasonable sum of money in 12 months, I pay a ridiculously large amount of tax. I resolve to learn from this for another tax year but fail miserably.

I continue to enjoy my work and have a balance between working for my small and imperfectly formed company and the European organization. I predict a downturn in internet fortunes for all but the most aggressive and persistent of companies. I identify my own company strengths and these do not include any aggression or persistence. Fortunately, help is on the horizon in the form of the organization as I ask to be employed full-time and they agree. The only downside I can see is that my own work will be reduced to almost nothing and the amount of time I have for 'building the business' will be zero. This is OK for now and I turn my full attention to developing this work. I enjoy meetings and I find that because of my education background, and more than passing interest in special needs, I can offer more than just technical suggestions at our meetings. My colleagues seem sensitive to my needs and way of working on the whole.

Good fortune abounds as I fulfil, rather belatedly, an ambition to get my PhD which I started when I was working in the university. When I was at school I was instructed to study Latin. I didn't opt for it, it was presented to me as a necessary subject for those who 'might be going on'. My school teachers often spoke in tongues to me. I realized later when I had gone through both chemistry and music transitions that I was identified as a potential Oxbridge type. It didn't appeal to me when I was at school. I don't know why, it just didn't. However, transferring some of my already completed work to a very accommodating and enlightened supervisor enabled me to be in receipt of the degree of PhD from Trinity College, Cambridge in something that as far as I am concerned (internet technologies in education) I am almost entirely self-taught in which I must confess I am quite proud of.

So, I have proven my competence at writing fairly long discourses on a singular, some might say, narrow topic. Sometimes, this extends to my online communications. I do find that my lengthy emails expressing my views on things are not always appreciated and that they do, sometimes, lead to misunderstandings. When these misunderstandings occur, I do wonder if I am always in the wrong. Perhaps I am. It is very difficult to tell but it is clear I have the capacity to misread situations. However, my good fortune in the world of work is really coming into its own as I work for a special needs education organization and if they don't understand the way I work nobody will. I'm bound to say that some of the decisions taken come as a surprise to me. I receive information about changes without very much notice sometimes and occasionally with no notice whatsoever.

This culminates in a meeting with no agenda (this is significant in the light of the next piece of information) when I am told my full-time services are no longer required (with one year of a five-year contract to run) and that I can have a part-time job (with a three-year contract) instead. I feel disappointed by the decision to do this to me. The reason I am given is that the financing of the organization has changed in its structure and that the rules around this require reductions in my type of job. I could be incorrect in my assessment of this situation but the fact I am not clear is probably significant.

I now need to go back in time before the meeting with no agenda in order to explain the background to this dramatic (for me) change which is slightly strange. I had enjoyed several years working full-time for this organization. Then, in the spring before the meeting with no agenda, there is a large meeting in the same place I went to for my interview. At this time, I am very happy with my position and my work. I remark upon this to my colleague who happens to be taking a short walk with me after a morning meeting. I go as far as to say that if I remain in this post until my retirement I will be more than happy. In an instant, there is momentary look on my colleague's face that tells me this is not to be. I await my fate. It takes several months for the next development in my career to be played out as I arrive in the winter of the same year when the meeting with no agenda takes place.

> Dilemma: In a few months I have a part-time job only. We have a mortgage and three children. What do I do?

> Outcome: [I am autistic.] I do know about autism so I could work in this field.

My wife points out that there is 'vacancy' of sorts in the autism outreach team she works for. I need to know a lot more about autism. I have some experience from a variety of opportunities and I start to 'cram' from the countless books around the house. I find it fascinating. This is slightly strange (even to me). My special interest has become autism. I absorb a library of books on all aspects of autism except the poetry. The poetry written by people with autism is not for me. I write it myself but only for amusement as a parody of 'that which should not be read' either out loud or to oneself. I once sat down and wrote 70 four-line poems.

I am fortunate in that my wife knows as much about the subject as anyone I have ever met and, I suspect, a good many of those I haven't. What makes her special (well there are actually so many things that even if I was into writing lists, which I'm not, it would be a very long list) is that she instinctively and intuitively applies this vast knowledge like no one else I either know or have read. For a neurotypical person, she has a profound understanding. Few neurotypical people I have met have this subtle blend of knowledge and practice and intuition. I can count them on the fingers of one hand. And it's the last bit, the intuition, that makes the blend special. Only a few people have it and even fewer employers.

I meet 'informally' with the team leader of an autism outreach service. My experience, skills and attitudes seem to be well received and I am genuinely excited by the prospects of doing some work with children with an autistic spectrum disorder (this is the current parlance). However, I am adamant that I do not have a disorder. I begin with a toe-dipping period of supply teaching. Then I complete a successful interview and my career has turned full circle and I am a part-time teacher in a centrally based service once again. There is an irony in this. Quite a lot of people have told me that I am a very intelligent person. So, have I under-achieved? In terms of status I suppose the answer is yes, yet the status of a job does not seduce me.

Those hungry for status in the world of work can manipulate people with Asperger Syndrome very easily. I know.

No one was or is my superior and I'm certainly not theirs. I only see colleagues in the workplace as doing different jobs that attract different rates of pay (sometimes unfairly so). Have I under-achieved in terms of pay? Again, I suppose the answer is yes, but so long as I can make an appropriate contribution to the care and support of my family and keep myself in electronic devices to make music with then I am comfortable with that. Have I under-achieved in terms of what I am capable of? Definitely, and I do feel frustrated by this. However, I have found that if you are not driven by status or pay, then realizing potential in the world of work as a neuro-diverse person is very difficult.

What drives me mad? The world of work thinking it is something special by making adjustments to accommodate people with autism. Isn't being a member of a team at least a two-way process? The way in which neuro-diverse people work is equally valid and sometimes more so. What is wrong with the world of work being set up for neuro-diverse people as well? Aren't some of the qualities highly desirable in the workplace? Many textbooks say this.

End bit

It might not have escaped the reader's attention that I have written least about my current employment. This is deliberate. Is the current job situation any different to the earlier experiences? Different yes, but it is still laden with challenges. Try holding down two part-time jobs in two distinctly different areas and that's only the start!

One of the most extraordinary things about my work with the outreach team is that I am treated like I have 'got better'. All my colleagues (I hope) understand that this is not possible. If they think that I can cope better with things, then they are right, I can. Is there a cost? You bet there is. All assumptions that I can manage without things like visual supports are, to some extent, correct. Would it help if I had them? Absolutely.

Can I cope with significant changes? Yes, to some extent I can. But the price I have to pay in anxiety and insecurity is still, and will remain, massive. I can mask this to some extent.

Do I need help in my work? Yes, I do and it is a remarkable piece of good fortune that my wife works in the same team. Should she need to help me? In an autism outreach team?

Do colleagues think that they can make decisions about what is best for people with autism? Yes, they do and for some of the time this is true. Do they think that seeking and embracing the views of somebody with autism is valuable? Not always, and sometimes rarely.

Could I go on? Of course I could, I have Asperger Syndrome. Would I have gainful employment? Probably not.

Reasonable adjustments? Yes, I think I've had to make a significant number.

Chapter 7: Finding, Applying For and Starting a Job

Mark Haggarty

Introduction by Luke Beardon
As other authors have debated so Mark raises the question of whether or not it is a good idea to disclose having AS on a CV or application form. Similarly, should one disclose when employed – and, if so, to whom? It is a difficult question as there is no single answer that will suit everyone. Some of the considerations include:

- *Will disclosure on an application form affect the chances of getting to interview? If so, then it may be better to avoid it at this stage.*

- *If you know that you will struggle at interview as a result of your AS it may be best to disclose prior to interview to help explain your methods of communicating and behaving. This is not to say use AS as any kind of excuse, rather an explanation of yourself.*

- *When in post consider the pros and cons of disclosure. Will it help in terms of your position, or is there a possibility of it being a negative?*

- *If you do decide to disclose it may be helpful to have an external party where possible who knows you well, who is willing and able to answer any questions employers/colleagues may have regarding AS.*

- *Remember, it is up to you whether or not you disclose, but you are protected by law – familiarize yourself with the relevant acts so that you know your legal position.*

I have tried to avoid to a large extent repeating things that can already be found in other books on the subject of seeking and succeeding in employment; I have tried to make what I write as relevant to the issues of Asperger Syndrome as possible, and what I say is based mostly on my own personal experiences and opinion rather than any hard research. I am not an expert on the topic and nor do I pretend to be one; rather I just try to give candid and honest advice based upon my own experiences as an individual with Asperger Syndrome who has spent ten years in employment. In writing this article I have had mainly what I would describe as the 'ordinary nine-to-five office-type job' in mind, although I would hope that I have given some accounts and ideas that could be applied to any type of employment.

Seeking employment

Even before contemplating the potential hardships associated with the workplace, for some individuals with Asperger Syndrome it can be a particular problem to actually secure a place of employment in the first place.

Of all the jobs that become available, many are never advertised. Various sources give differing statistics, but it is probably true to say that this accounts for between 50 and 75 per cent of all positions. Instead they are filled through word of mouth alone. This may be another disadvantage for those of us with Asperger Syndrome as we may be less likely to have the necessary contacts to enable us to become aware of these positions and to therefore have a chance of being considered for one of them.

The first stage is to actually find a position for which you would like to apply and to be offered a job interview. There are a number of books available and sites on the internet which give advice on how to complete a CV, and how to seek and apply for a new job; take some time to search for and make use of these materials – they will outline the dos and don'ts of job searching. The material that is available may seem daunting and overwhelming, and sometimes conflicting, so do get a family member or friend to help you and guide you through the whole process if you can. Although the internet contains many sites on the topic of job searching, it may be better to find one or two good books on the topic and concentrate on them.

If you are thinking of responding to an advertisement for a particular position, it may be worthwhile getting in touch with the relevant contact person at the organization to which you are applying and having an informal talk to inform them that you are interested in the position that they are advertising, and to find out more about the position yourself, rather than jumping straight in and submitting a formal application. Some companies may also be willing to let you pay an informal visit their office so that you can chat about the position and see where you would potentially be working. This is good not only because it conveys your enthusiasm, but it will allow you to get a feeling for the place, and it will not be totally unfamiliar if you return there for an interview. It will also enable you to assess whether you think it would be a comfortable working environment for you. If you perceive for whatever reason that you really would not be comfortable working in that particular workplace, you may be better off walking away at that stage and looking elsewhere – it could be very frustrating for you if you walk into an office for the very first time for your first day of work, only to find that you really dislike the workspace because of issues such as noises or strong fluorescent lighting!

If you are going to respond to a job advertisement, find out as much as you can about the organization to which you will be applying. Begin with simple things such as when the company was established, how many people they employ and exactly what type of business they are involved in. Knowing this information should make the process that is to follow less daunting and it will give you an idea as to whether the organization will make a suitable workplace for you. As well as that, it will also mean that you can show a certain degree of knowledge about the company should you go for an interview. It is never a good idea to go to a job interview without any knowledge of the company you could potentially be going to work for!

If, ultimately, you find that your efforts to research the company are not turning up much information, you could even phone the company up and state that you are possibly interested in applying for employment there and ask them directly for some information about them.

If there is also any way that you can get an account from a person who already works for the organization of what it is like, and what they do and don't like about working there, so much the better, although this may be difficult if you don't have any relevant contacts to assist with this.

The interview

I am sure that you will agree that it is somewhat unjust that many people with Asperger Syndrome have difficulty in gaining a place in employment, as we are perfectly capable of doing many jobs. Let's face it, the typical job interview is not so much an assessment of how well you will actually do the job for which you are applying, rather it is an assessment on how well you present yourself and cope with job interviews. It is somewhat unfair that a mere 30-minute conversation determines whether or not you will be offered the opportunity to work for an organization. Your prospective employers can hardly tell how well you will perform in the role from this 30-minute discussion. It is ultimately during the first few months in the post that you demonstrate (or not) your suitability for the position, but you first have to triumph in that distorted process which is the job interview in order to win that opportunity. As unreasonable as it may seem, that is the way that things are done and so one has to do one's best at it.

Difficulties at the interview stage are undoubtedly one of the main reasons why some people with Asperger Syndrome struggle to gain employment. If this is the case for you, you must therefore do everything you possibly can to give you the best chance of securing that job when you go into that interview room. If necessary, that means NOT being yourself and putting on rather more of an act! I am not suggesting for one second that you should go in there and feed your interviewers with falsehoods about yourself and your abilities; that is an absolute no no! Rather, you have to say what they want to hear whilst remaining truthful, act in a manner that they want to see and also present yourself as having an agreeable personality. Many individuals with Asperger Syndrome may not be the best advocate of their own strengths, and may be overly reserved and modest in talking about those strengths to others, especially those individuals that are the quiet and introverted type. If you think that this is a problem for you, you need to train yourself to act vociferously and talk about your strengths with confidence (but without seeming cocky)! You must also avoid saying things that your interviewers don't want to hear. Just as you will most likely be asked about your strengths, some interviewers may ask directly what you consider to be your weaknesses. A typical

Asperger Syndrome response would be to give a thoughtful and honest response as to what you consider your weaknesses to be. Whilst some interviewers may appreciate such flagrant honesty, this may not be the best approach in all circumstances. An alternative approach could be to mention something which could actually be considered a strength, but construe it to sound as if it is a weakness. If it is unclear what I mean by this, here are a couple of examples. You could say that you tend to get overly absorbed and stuck into the task in hand which makes you lose track of the time sometimes. Another possibility is to say that you tend to drag yourself into work come what may even when you are unwell and should perhaps be staying at home. If you don't think that you can manage to think of any examples which mix together the positive and negative aspect in one trait in this way, mention your weaknesses, but always follow them up with a 'but' and then mention some of your strengths. Remember, although you obviously should be entirely truthful in your presentation of yourself, you don't have to tell them everything!

If you are applying for a position which is related to a particular interest of yours, avoid stultifying your interviewers with a lengthy disquisition (as I did once)! Although it is always good to show knowledge, it won't do you any favours to overdo it! It may seem uncomfortable putting on such an act if it is not your usual personality, but it is only for half an hour or so, which is nevertheless a half hour that may secure you a job which you could possibly hold for a number of years, so it is worthwhile making sure that you get it right!

Be aware that those scrutinizers who interview you will be covertly studying you and assessing you in every minute detail, observing body language as well as listening to what you say. The fact that, to them, your body language may be an important factor in how they perceive you may be unfortunate for some individuals with Asperger Syndrome. My experience is that if you are unsure how your body language will be perceived, the less, the better. Try to make a conscious effort to keep your entire body still, whilst still being relaxed. Place your hands together on your lap or rest them on the table in front of you, and avoid making gestures or waving your arms about! If you do, you may be inadvertently giving subliminal messages that you are uncomfortable with the situation you are currently in, and you may detract from what you are saying. If you keep still, the emphasis will be on what you are saying rather than on what you are doing, and the interviewers should be unable to derive anything negative!

Unfortunately you can never be sure exactly what questions you will be asked during a job interview, therefore it is not possible to plan in advance exactly what you will say. However, you will certainly perform much better if you are well prepared. Consider what strengths or abilities that you possess which you can promote when the opportunity presents itself, and although you can never predict what you will be asked, it is definitely worth preparing answers to a few broad questions which will probably come up. Common questions in job interviews include:

- Tell us a bit about yourself.
- Why do you want to work for us?
- What can you offer our organization?
- What are your strengths?

It can be tough for some people with Asperger Syndrome to come up with instantaneous answers to these questions if they have not thought about them in advance.

Even though it shouldn't be a problem for most people to tell someone about themselves without needing to prepare in advance what they will say, I find that you will be more relaxed and present yourself better if you have thought in advance about what you are going to say, rather than having to instantly think about what you are saying in what is after all a tense situation.

Ask your family for help in deciding how you would respond to these questions. My one piece of top advice is to ask them also what they think your strengths are – they may have a much better idea than you!

Job interviews are discussed further in the next section.

Should you tell your employer and your colleagues?

Whether you tell people about your Asperger Syndrome is of course entirely your own decision which should be appropriate to your own feelings and circumstances; however, I would like talk about my own experiences and beliefs which will hopefully give you some guidance in making that decision should you be unsure.

I personally do not think that it is a great idea to mention it on your CV, or you risk putting off some ill-informed employers at the very first stage! I believe that when you seek employment, no matter how much of a big deal you feel that your Asperger Syndrome is to you in your general life, and whatever complications you anticipate it will cause for you in the work-place, you have the right to be assessed as an individual person who has their own unique strengths and shortcomings just like anybody. Whether those strengths or shortcomings are as a result of having Asperger Syndrome is beside the point. Whether or not you decide to introduce the words 'Asperger Syndrome' into the equation during your job-seeking process and at what point you decide to do so is something for you to decide based upon whether you feel it is appropriate to do so, but I certainly don't believe that you should feel obliged to do so. Let your potential employers assess you, not your Asperger Syndrome.

If you have attended a number of job interviews but you believe that you are being discounted by prospective employers because you are displaying some eccentricity during the job interview, it may be worth considering raising the subject during future interviews. If you have not had any luck in securing a job so far because of poor interview performance, there isn't really anything to lose and you may need to try the approach of discussing Asperger Syndrome with your interlocutors so at least they will have a better understanding of you and you should then have a better chance. If you do choose to raise the subject during an interview, do, however, make sure that you convey some of the positive attributes associated with the condition which would be desirable to your prospective employer. Just in case you need some ideas, here's a few positive Asperger Syndrome traits – consider if any of these describe you: showing attention to detail; not getting easily distracted from the task in hand; being punctual, proactive, perfectionist, careful, accurate; having a dislike of breaking rules… I am sure that there are more but I am struggling to think of them!

If there is no aspect of your Asperger Syndrome which causes any significant impediment in the workplace, and you exhibit no behaviours that could indicate to your colleagues that you are anything other than neurotypical (or even if you do), it may be that you would prefer never to mention it and not let it be relevant to your work life. You may just want to come to work each day, do your job and then go home just like everyone else. This is understandable, considering many people still know little about Asperger Syndrome. Some may have heard the term but know little about it. Many will not have even heard of it. Because of this, you may understandably feel some apprehension about wanting to talk to your colleagues about it, for fear that it may give some less judicious people a tainted opinion of you. There may be some worry that your work life will be adversely changed and that you will never properly fit in if you tell everyone that you have Asperger Syndrome.

However, I believe that there is a great deal of benefit to letting colleagues know, and that you will be better understood and accepted if you do. If your colleagues know nothing about Asperger Syndrome, you must educate them. If you work in a large office, it may be that you would be more comfortable telling just a small group of persons with whom you work most closely rather than everybody, but either way, I believe that you will ultimately be better off if you tell somebody rather than never mentioning it.

If you still have worries about making people aware, consider this: I have worked in places where there have been members of staff with cerebral palsy, members of staff who are amputees and members of staff who are wheelchair bound. Although you can't help but ruminate over it for a short while after you first become acquainted with such a person, it soon thereafter becomes the norm and you no longer even think about it. In the same way there is no reason why telling your colleagues that you have Asperger Syndrome should make it a major day-to-day issue in your workplace from then on. It just means that if you happen to display apparently eccentric behaviour, your colleagues will understand why. For example, if you do not feel comfortable socializing with your colleagues too much outside the scope of work-related matters and hence you generally avoid such situations, your colleagues will know to put it down to your Asperger Syndrome if they are aware of it and then they will think nothing more of it. If, however, your colleagues are not aware of your Asperger Syndrome, they may believe that you are anti-social and egocentric if you decline invitations, and this could taint their perception of you, which could in turn have ramifications for your relationship with them in the workplace.

Telling your employer will also allow you to address any issues that you may have with your working environment from a sensory perspective, as you can then discuss with them what could be done to make things more comfortable for you.

The benefits of revealing your Asperger Syndrome (at least to immediate colleagues) outweigh any ramifications, so unless you are absolutely determined that you don't want anyone to know about it, do discuss it with your colleagues. Even if you are determined to keep it quiet, please do reconsider!

Day to day in the workplace

If you possess the laudable Asperger Syndrome trait of being bluntly honest and forthright at all times, be careful! It is not always necessarily a good thing in the workplace.

On a couple of previous occasions when a group of external auditors have visited the office where I work to review some financial statements, my manager has had to discreetly remind me before they arrive that I need to be careful what I say to them, and that means just answering their questions in a clear and succinct manner, and certainly not offer any information unless they ask for it! There were instances before that when I would sit down with the auditors and imprudently tell them about every error and stuff-up that had occurred, and point out to them every minor discrepancy that could be found in what they were auditing! I would quite happily spend a good few minutes doing this, all the time unaware of the horrified looks on my manager's face!

On a lighter note, I think that my colleagues find me mildly amusing in that they know that if they ask me how I am, or if they ask me what I think of something they are wearing, they will get an honest answer!

If you sometimes experience sensory issues or just simply feel overloaded at work, think is there is anything that could be done to make your workspace more comfortable for you, and discuss things with your employer. This could be requesting to be positioned next to a window so as to get as much natural light as possible. Personally, I hate arriving at work and walking into a busy, crowded office. I like to commence work quite early in the morning, as it is nice to be the first to arrive in the office at 7.30 a.m. as it means that I can work in peace and without distraction for a while! The commotion gradually builds up as people arrive and it has less of an overwhelming impact than walking straight into a busy office at nine o'clock! If you can relate to this, then seeing if you can arrange slightly different working hours may be worthwhile.

It has often surprised me how some people only spend as little as a few days in a new job before deciding to leave because they do not like it. How anyone can make a determination that they do not want to continue in a job in such a short period of time is something that I cannot comprehend.

When you begin work in a new job, even if your initial experiences are not particularly positive, I believe that you need to spend at least six months in the job, ideally a year, before you can be sure whether or not it is not right for you.

When you begin a new job, whatever you do, do not become demoralized if things are initially tough. Stick it out. As you become settled in, things tend to improve with time and you will adapt to your new workplace. When I changed jobs after spending more than five years with one organization, I thought that I had made a terrible mistake. Different people, different rules, tougher work, overall different mentality. I thought that I would never stand a chance of learning and remembering all the new things that I needed to know to do my new job. However, no matter how difficult the work may seem at first, and no matter how difficult you find it to interact with your colleagues, things do get easier with time.

If ultimately you do decide that a particular job is not for you and you don't want to continue with it, restart your job searching process, but try to stay with your current job and do not resign until you have been offered and accepted a new job. Any time spent in any job is experience which is worthwhile.

Remember, when you are working for someone else, no job will be perfect. If you do find a perfect job where there is absolutely nothing that frustrates you, then you are very lucky. There will always be some aspect of the work, the workplace or the ways of your employer that annoys you. That is unfortunately something that one must live with. Weigh up the good points and the bad points in your mind, and if there is more right with your job than there is wrong with it, think carefully before throwing it all away.

Relationships with colleagues

How well you get along with your work colleagues is probably the most influential factor in determining how content you will be in a job. Unfortunately, it seems that personality clashes are a facet of working with other people, and there will very often be at least one person who inexplicably appears to take a dislike to you!

Do try to remain agreeable at all times if you can! A busted fax machine when I was expecting a very important communication one time was enough to send me into an uncontrollable fit of rage! If something is making you agitated, whether it is a person or a faulty piece of equipment or software, take five minutes to step outside and breathe some fresh air and regain your composure. If you are in a capricious state of mind it would not be the best thing to end up getting totally wound up to the extent that you take your frustrations out on somebody else.

I will close on what is intended to be a reassuring note. Just remember that in most cases, any person with whom you do not seem to be able to get along with particularly well will not bear any personal animosity towards you, it is more likely that as a person with Asperger Syndrome you may be misinterpreting their behaviour as being more impudent than it actually is, and that there is just simply an 'incompatibility' between you. If that is not the case, chances are that the person treats everybody in the same way and that nobody else particularly likes them either – if that is so you will soon find out!

Chapter 8: What I have Learned from 25 Years of Employment

Steve Jarvis

Introduction by Luke Beardon

Steve makes an excellent point early on in this chapter regarding the lack of self-awareness that he felt contributed to poor decisions regarding his own employment. I think that this is something that is just as important to recognize for employers as it is for the employees. If an employer employs someone with AS all credit to them – but they should not automatically expect the individual to know what support structures need to be put in place. It should be the responsibility just as much, if not more so, of the employer to work out how best to support their staff, and they should not simply rely on the individual with AS to come up with support mechanisms. Sure, it may not be an easy thing to do – but the rewards gained from a successful work placement may well make the effort worthwhile.

I would like to share with you what I have learned from 25 years of employment. Perhaps my experience and lessons learned may be of some help to you. I was only diagnosed with Asperger Syndrome in 2006 at the age of 45. I know that I am fortunate to have been able to hold down a full-time job for most of my adult life.

At college I gained much satisfaction from doing one-to-one tutoring in mathematics. It was this that made me decide to train to be a teacher. With hindsight this was a very poor decision. I did not have the awareness to see that managing a class of teenage kids would be very stressful for me. My probationary year was a miserable experience, and I started to abuse alcohol at this time. I realize now that I lacked the communication and social skills to interact effectively with the children and my poor emotional awareness was also a major obstacle. The advice I would like to share with you is this. I think that the lack of self-awareness in many people with Asperger Syndrome can make it difficult to make good decisions when it comes to choice of employment. I failed to consider my poor emotional and social skills in deciding to be a teacher, because I was not aware that I had poor skills in these areas. I would recommend seeking professional help in making this important decision from people who appreciate the particular difficulties faced by us Aspies. I understand that there are now specialist employment services for people with autism and Asperger Syndrome.

I left the teaching profession to become a software engineer. This was a much better decision. However, I was still very unhappy and I wrongly thought this was to do with my job rather than difficulties that stemmed from being on the autistic spectrum. On two separate occasions in my twenties and thirties I sought professional careers advice. I was given personality and psychometric tests and a counselling session, and these helped to raise my awareness of my strengths and weaknesses. I think psychometric tests are useful for people on the autistic spectrum, because the information is presented in a helpful form that is easier to accept than from friends or family.

I realize now that I was learning all the time how to function at work and to manage the high levels of stress associated with having to interact regularly with other people. I would say that the single most powerful technique that I have developed to help with this is rigorous planning and preparation. I am aware that planning and time management are not easy skills to learn for people with Asperger Syndrome. Every day I maintain a task list. I work out what is the most important and urgent task to do. If I am uncertain, I will ask my manager. I now use Microsoft Outlook to maintain my task list electronically. Before every meeting I think out the purpose of the meeting and how I should approach it. Planning cannot prepare you for all possible eventualities, but I find it helps me to maintain my confidence in situations that I cannot control. I am frequently much more prepared than my colleagues. The downside of rigorous planning is that I am not as productive as other people.

Before my diagnosis, I continued to make unwise decisions in career changes. I failed to realize that whenever I took on more management responsibility, I struggled with the increased need to achieve goals through interacting with other people. My lack of emotional and social skills meant that I had to think things through logically and this was not always possible in social situations.

After my positive diagnosis, the psychologist who assessed me gave me a letter that I could use to explain Asperger Syndrome to my employer. I anguished for a long time as to whether I should disclose at work. In the end I decided to only disclose to my immediate boss and one other colleague who had been giving me most support. I felt that they deserved to know why I struggled so badly in certain areas of my work. I gave a customized version of this employer letter to these two people. I strongly recommend the use of such a letter as a communication tool. I have included an extract from my letter that I hope illustrates this.

'...More specifically, Steve has outlined to me the kind of difficulties he has and how these may be overcome with support. Steve has informed me how grateful he is for the level of support he receives from you, and that he feels that it is time that you had an explanation for the need for this support.

DECISION-MAKING
Steve finds some decision-making a challenge and this can result in an appearance of being slow to act and also lead to unnecessarily detailed explanations. He values the opportunity to check his decisions with others to gain reassurance that they are sound.

INAPPROPRIATE LEVEL OF COMMUNICATION
Steve is aware that he sometimes provides too much information, and that this may be seen as not an efficient use of time. He appreciates the explicit instructions that you provide.

SOCIAL INTERACTION

Steve finds certain kinds of social interaction difficult and stressful (e.g. meeting many strangers at one time and confrontation). His eye contact can be poor if he is feeling a lack of confidence. He has disclosed to me that he tries to avoid too many situations like this in a working week.

MEETINGS

Steve finds meetings with large numbers of people can be a challenge, because of the unpredictable nature of communications. He likes to gain control and this explains why he feels the need to prepare and plan thoroughly for important meetings.

POLITICS AND HIDDEN AGENDAS

Steve finds it difficult to appreciate office politics and other people's hidden agendas. Where this exists and is important, it is helpful to check with Steve that he has appreciated the underlying motives of others for their behaviour and actions.

LACK OF CONFIDENCE

The difficulties described above can result in an apparent lack of confidence and self-belief. Steve appreciates positive feedback when he does something well, particularly in the challenging areas, but equally he values constructive feedback when expected levels of performance are not achieved.

A positive aspect that Steve has shared with me is his belief that he is quick learner and with an eye for detail that sometimes is important in his role...'

Conclusions and recommended reading

I am happier now at work, because I know that I will get the support I need. I still find full-time employment a source of much stress and anxiety. I use various relaxation techniques to help reduce unhealthy levels of stress. My favourite is progressive relaxation that involves tensing muscles in the body. I would like to recommend the following workbook:

Davis, M., McKay, M. and Robbins Eshelman, E. (2000) *The Relaxation and Stress Reduction Workbook*, fifth edition. New York: New Harbinger Publications, Inc.

If you are considering employment that involves management as someone with Asperger Syndrome, I can also recommend the book by Malcolm Johnson, below. I have regularly referred to Johnson's advice on preparation for meetings and he also has useful points to make on office politics. I struggle most when I find myself working with people who are emotionally volatile and use their intuition and emotions to make their decisions. These are often the people who can be manipulative. It is not always possible to avoid such people, but I would recommend trying to avoid working with them as they can be a considerable source of stress and worry at work.

Johnson, M. (2005) *Managing with Asperger Syndrome: A Practical Guide For White Collar Professionals*. London: Jessica Kingsley Publishers.

Chapter 9: Asperger Syndrome and Employment: My Experiences and Observations

Anne Henderson

Introduction by Luke Beardon

I really like the optimism shown at the end of this piece. It would be great to think that Anne's experience, and her son's, is one that will not have to be endured by other parents or individuals in the future. Sadly, this may not be the case. Although legislation has improved, and knowledge and understanding are gradually becoming more widespread, the general population still have a long way to go until individuals with AS are truly accepted and supported. In the mean time, then, what can be done? For individuals with AS currently employed I think it is essential to ensure proper support is in place, using the law as leverage if need be. For individuals currently seeking employment, take advice from other individuals who are experienced in supporting people with AS. Online support groups could be a great way for this – Aspie Village (www.aspievillage.org.uk, accessed 15 January 2008) is an excellent place to start. Alternatively seek 'professional' guidance, but always be aware that you may have a better understanding of AS than many of the people you seek advice from!

My son has Asperger Syndrome which was not diagnosed until he was in his late twenties and that was about ten years ago – long after he had left school and had tried extremely hard to succeed in employment and earn his own living. He knows that I am writing this and is happy for me to do so if it helps illustrate how difficult employment can be for someone with Asperger's.

School must have been a nightmare for him as he received no help and he had to cope without any recognition of his special needs or support. He left school at 15 and from there went on a YTS (Youth Training Scheme) where he learnt a bit of woodwork and a few catering skills but he was desperately unhappy and lonely – it was a very unhappy time for him as he found mixing with his peers even more difficult than he had at school. The social interaction that people not on the spectrum learn automatically and take for granted became even more complex in a work situation. It must have been exhausting for him to try and make sense of this new situation but he persevered and, with plenty of coaching, was accepted to do a horticultural course at his local college, with work experience. He was to be supported by a trust which helps people find work and his work placement was with a small company who maintained grounds for residential/old peoples' homes etc. This company was funded by a charity which helps vulnerable people with work placements and a variety of grants.

I don't remember all the details but know that he was happy to be working and he was part of a team of three – the foreman and one other man. It was the best introduction to work as the foreman was patient and understood how people with AS need clear direction and time to process instructions, also it was a very small team.

There are one or two things that that really stick in my mind, the first was after my son had opened his bank account and went to withdraw money. He was inconsolable as he kept asking for the pound notes that he had deposited and insisted that the money he was given was not his. His sister was with him and it was only after they had talked that we realized that the notes that he had withdrawn had different serial numbers to those he had deposited!

The second was an incident that could have had disastrous consequences – he had progressed to using a strimmer and all went well until there was a slightly different area to be strimmed and the strimmer jammed and caught fire. The result of this different set of circumstances caused panic and my son's coat caught fire. However, it shows how difficult it is for him if suddenly faced with a totally different set of circumstances, i.e. the strimmer not behaving in the usual way and in a different place.

Apart from a few ups and downs work and college progressed well and it was a difficult time when the funding for the company dried up and everyone had to find new employment. This change was particularly unsettling but, with help from the trust, most of the employees transferred to a very large contractor and that was very difficult for my son – the change was enormous and difficult for anyone, let alone someone with AS.

The new employers were a huge national gardening contractor with contracts to maintain parks, municipal gardens and a cemetery, and do groundwork at nursing homes, homes for the elderly where my son had worked previously. At first all went well but because he was unable to follow instructions which he clearly did not understand he was labelled as a bolshie employee and became the butt of jokes and scapegoat for everything that went wrong.

I do not want to dwell on this but all he wanted to do was work and fit in but he became more and more aware of his differences and some people can be incredibly cruel to anyone different. The stress began to have an effect on his mental health – he was eventually dismissed over an incident where he did not understand an instruction and pruned the wrong shrubs!

After this incident he immediately found himself another gardening job with a large company working as part of a team maintaining the grounds, but by this time his isolation became a real problem and he was admitted to hospital as a result of his anxiety. This must have been so hard for him as all he had been trying to do was to be like everyone else and work and earn his own living and be part of society.

After this stay he was eventually diagnosed with Asperger Syndrome and started a college course with tutors who supported him. He was successful in his studies but there was no follow-up support and there was another unsuccessful attempt at employment. He found another job working for a supermarket stacking shelves on the night shift – again the problem was dealing with changes in routine and mixing with other staff. The supermarket management were extremely supportive to the extent of getting the National Autistic Society to explain AS to several of their managers. However, the job was to cause so much anxiety that he started to become unwell again – just stacking the cornflakes in a different place was enough to throw him and he found the noise and hustle and bustle of customers when he moved to days just too much to deal with. It was decided that it was not the right environment for him and he left. He tried and tried to find work – data entry, washing up, anything and everything – but without success and he became more and more disillusioned and eventually gave up. He was sectioned and spent three years in a forensic secure ward.

So many of the problems he has faced have been as a result of ignorance and lack of awareness of the differences between those with AS and those without. People with AS have incredible talents to bring to employment but the trick is to find the right job and right place and to turn an interest into an asset and to understand the differences, particularly in communication.

To end on a positive note, my son is at college doing an IT course, again with proper support and living in a house with others with AS and staffed by people who are ASD friendly – he has just been nominated as Student of the Year in his class in a mainstream college so it proves what can be achieved with the right support. And finally, things are beginning to change for Asperger's individuals to improve their quality of life.

10: What Aspies Need to Know When Working in the Neurotypical Environment

Cornish

Introduction by Luke Beardon

In this chapter there are some strong opinions expressed which are as a direct result of Cornish's life experience. While this may make for uncomfortable reading it must be noted that the purpose of this book is to allow a genuine platform for adults with AS to speak out; in addition, we hope that this book will reduce negative experiences such as Cornish's for other people with AS by educating the general population to the best of our ability. Please remember that this is one individual's experience and perspective, and is not necessarily representative of all people with AS or, indeed, the NT population. However, it is a genuine opinion and with the appropriate understanding as to why this opinion has arisen (i.e. resulting from his experiences as a person with AS in the NT environment) no offence should be taken. How Cornish has managed to go through the life he has without losing it completely is beyond me — but then again, people with AS are full of surprises, many of them extremely refreshing and positive!

OK, this is my own and very individual take on working within the NT environment. I'm not promising anything pretty, and I don't know how easy it will be for some people to accept, but it is my experiences and my conclusions, and I'm making no apologies for my thoughts on this. To all you aspiring Aspies out there: read carefully and inwardly digest. To all NTs reading this: time to get real. Wake up and start doing the right thing.

I'll start with a bit of wisdom and then some 'potted history' then I'll get to the point, and give you the benefit of my experience. But before I start I would like you all to bear in mind that what you read has been directly 'coloured' by my past treatment of practically every individual I've encountered, and so, I'll begin.

The secret of a happy and fulfilling Aspergian life is to first know and understand your individual limits and boundaries; second, you have to fully accept these limitations, and then stick to living your life within these boundaries. Anything else and you will be setting yourself up for failure...be warned...get realistic.

So, to be able to achieve this, it is essential that you learn as much as possible about Asperger Syndrome. See how much applies to you and then identify your strengths and weaknesses. I understand that this may not always be easy for some Aspergians, and for many who don't have appro- priate support around them, and, especially if they have had too many negative experiences in their past, their outlook on life may be their greatest hindrance. For these Aspies, find yourself an AS-specific counsel- lor – get sorted. They are not common, but search them out – and they will be the best form of self-investment you can have. For myself, the more I learned about AS, the more I understood *me*. Through this I began to realize, that from having existed within a living nightmare for 40-odd years, I was now in possession of one of the rarest gifts on the planet! Filling in the 'blanks' has been one of the most enlightening and self-empowering episodes in my life. Once I had access to the right infor- mation, I could start to become who I really was. Since my diagnosis in 2003, people have asked me if I've become more Aspie – I reply that I've become less NT, and that's about right.

The other aspect to Aspergian life is to learn about the other 'side of the coin'. The more you learn about the neurotypical genotype, then the more you will understand the nature of their world in contrast to our own.

And make no mistake...the two worlds are very different.

But with an intimate understanding, and again, acceptance (not always easy), it is possible for the two genetic profiles to work together in some situations.

So, a brief history

My time at school was one of a neverending nightmare for 11 years. So the thought of spending my next 50 years in more or less the same environment, i.e. a working one, pushed me close to suicide.

My only aspiration on leaving school was to opt out of mainstream for good. But back in the 1970s this was never going to be an option that mainstream society would allow – and I was fully aware of this.

At 16 I was socially, emotionally and mentally immature for my years. So as well as all of the other impairments that come with Asperger Syndrome, it meant that I was crippled as soon as I stepped out on to the street to the point of non-functionality. To then be thrown into an environment that was populated in the main by mature adults (mainly males), all with a mentality of work-centred priorities, left me lost and residing in a state of utter despair. Just like at school, I was being forced into doing things, and being in places that felt completely unnatural. It always felt like I was being forced into a mental concentration camp. I simply could not cope with such an intense neurotypical environment. Basically I was being asked to grow gills.

This also reinforced my feelings of never fitting in, and this only served to concentrate my feelings of isolation.

I also knew that, logically, if I found work locally, then there would be every chance I would find myself working alongside people who had constantly bullied me for the previous 11 years. Again, the thought of this had me planning suicide for most of my days. The thought of 50 more years of abject misery, 10 or 20 years of retirement if you are lucky, and then you die, to my way of thinking, was both futile and pointless. I could save myself a lot of trauma by just ending my life!

What was equally distressing, was that the workforce of the nation found this form of social incarceration totally acceptable! The gulf between my understanding of my world and theirs was just too wide, and to be forced into a soul-destroying way of life made no sense to me at all – and – there didn't seem to be any escape from it.

Like many on the autistic spectrum, I only knew how to run from a terrible situation, with little thought of where I was running to. With having a distinct lack of predictive imagination, it's no wonder I ran into an even worse environment. The NT phrase 'out of the frying pan into the fire' was very applicable. On leaving school, I made a career choice which, for some reason, I thought would be the best way of avoiding the bullies (I won't name the employer specifically here)...but I was WRONG!!!

Although the local bullies had been left behind, in my naivety I had not realized that bullies were everywhere and anywhere I went. I just hadn't the Theory of Mind to understand this.

Once again an absolute nightmare. In this 'lads' lad' of a place, I had no idea of what being a 'team' player was, and what was required of me. On board a ship full of 'blerks', I was still an absolute loner, and still having the life bullied out of me. This was an intensely 'blerky' environment, where I was a total alien living amongst them.

After one such trip to Rio de Janeiro, I was emotionally, mentally and physically exhausted. I felt I had no choice but to desert; and so I went a.w.o.l. After two weeks I ran out of money, and had to return to a very surprised ship's company. I went up in front of the ship's captain, who very reasonably informed me that we were setting off for Australia, and if I was feeling just as distressed when we got there, then he would fly me home from Sydney. When we got there, I told him my condition hadn't changed and I was ready to go home now. To my utter dismay his exact words were:

'Surely, you didn't really believe we would fly you back?'

Everything went black as I passed out on the spot.

In my Aspergian naivety, I had been gullible enough to take him at his word. I kind of mentally went off the rails after that and after another six months at sea, and much to my parents' disappointment, I was released from the grasp of that employer on our return to England.

Back home at my parents', I was faced with the same dilemma. After again being bullied non-stop in that job — coupled this time with sexual assaults — I was asking the question...'How could I stop this happening again?' This was 1978 and I couldn't see any positions for hermits in the Job Centre. My parents put me under pressure to get a job as soon as I had left the last one, but no one understood what I was going through, nobody — I didn't understand — no one knew about Asperger Syndrome in those days, and again I found myself trapped in a world where I didn't belong.

I had no understanding of the social concepts...of going out into the world and making something of myself. I had never grasped the abstract concept of ambition or goal setting. I had no interest in money or the acquisition of goods or family or property. Once again I couldn't work out the reasons why people did what they did. All I wanted was to be left alone.

Soon, and under due protest, I was once again back in the grown-up world of men where I had been taken on at a local plastics manufacturing factory. Once again I was shut away inside a depressing soul-destroying situation that for no sane reason I could fathom. Again I couldn't cope. I had to get out. I had to find some way of existing in a world that consistently made me unwelcome; and again I was bullied out of that job, I eventually left and adopted the ways of the Beats and hippies... I was trying to find peace.

1982. The early Thatcher years, and thankfully, high unemployment. I don't mean to be disrespectful, but what a Godsend. Up until now, unbeknown to me, I had been suffering with the inflexibility of thought and the inability to adapt to another person's way of doing things so common in Aspergian people. The inability to relate to others, having different priorities in the world and simply being a completely different 'animal' to everyone around me, always left me in dire straits...also at that time, I thought I was the only one like me on the planet...all the way up until my diagnosis.

I had moved into my own place by then, and had taken as much control over my life as possible. I vowed never to put myself in such vulnerable positions again. I identified everything that caused me grief in my life, and removed it...from now on everything would be on my terms...no more bullying...no more misery... I stepped out of mainstream society with no intention to return...27 years on, I still haven't...well, not quite...

So that is my story, I would hope yours has been somewhat different, somewhat happier. This next stuff is my best conclusion of my experience, I think it's a fair representation of what is...take heed...from my bubble to yours...

OK, here we go: if you really want to step outside of your little autistic bubble, if you really want to go out there and join the mass immersion of the working masses, if you really want that job – you had better understand just what you are getting yourself into. You need to know what sort of environment the NTs have created for themselves so far as the workplace is concerned, and how they play their little games of 'getting on in life'. If you really want to take part in this whole insane shebang of 'social incarceration', then you need to wise up. If you are not prepared for what you are entering into, then it will, with certain guarantee, all turn round and in the blink of an eye, screw your shit up good and proper. Make no mistake, it will turn around and bite you on your naive, innocent squeaky AS ass!

This is the high-pressure treadmill of competitive 'king of the hill', of oneupmanship, and who can climb over who in the race to the top. Where petty little empires are won and lost. This is the world of small time personal politics, and the big world of the so-called adult conspiracy. In reality – this is the world that the NTs have taken thousands of years to make. This is their product. This is the world of exploitation, where, if you are an employee, your employer will get more out of you than you will out of them. Seldom is this a mutual arrangement. If you go self-employed, then market forces will be conspiring to help you crash and burn. Unless you do a Bill Gates, and you have almost paranormal powers, can read the zeitgeist and then become the wealthiest man on the planet – it is impossible for Aspergians to beat the NTs at their own game.

If you are to stand any chance out there, you need to understand what sort of 'animal' the NTs are. If you are to stand any chance at all, you need to know how to out-NT the NTs. I can't tell you everything you need to know here because a lot of this depends on experience and the understanding that these people are generally self-serving with their own personal agendas. So never mind this integrating teamwork thing, the dog-eat-dog principle is always in force. Just as it was pointed out to me at a recent self-employment seminar – 'Get out there, and get them before breakfast!'

If you think all of this is somewhat melodramatic, then WAKE UP! The truth is, that the majority of the people you will be working with will be small-minded, sociopathic, intolerant bigots, probably with IQs a lot lower than your own. NTs expect bullshit, so learn how to talk it – forget about being honest, this will get you nowhere. NTs have no sense of probity, and wouldn't know the truth if it came and bit them in the ass. They will never tell you what they are thinking and they don't expect it from you, so don't bother: they would be more likely to engage in the undermining of some unsuspecting sap whose position they have probably envied for a time. This is quite normal, there is always the game of superiority over inferiority going on, just make sure you are not the target by doing your job too well and showing everyone up. Like the rest of your work colleagues, only do as much as you can get away with – nothing more than that.

If you are one of these 'we can all live in harmony' Aspies, then quite frankly, somewhere along the line you will be 'had for breakfast'. This 'let's all get along together' doesn't work with NTs, it will only ever be a 'nice' sentiment. This bullshit is for 'cloud cuckoo landers', whose lack of Theory of Mind is so severe, that they just don't suspect there's anything to suspect. Only rarely in my experience is the AS/NT mix conducive and mutual; and believe me, the NT world is full of hidden agendas that are there to put you at a disadvantage. When you can't tell the good guys from the bad guys, and the fact that the average 'normal' person tells 20 'white lies' a day according to Professor Robert Winston, it is hard to trust any situation you may find yourself in... Oh, and don't forget, the majority of people don't particularly like the jobs they are in. So, if you are one of the few lucky Aspergians that have managed to turn your specialist interest into an occupation, then you are indeed a unique individual. It also means you probably work on your own!

So the first thing you need to realize if you want to work along side NTs is: most of them work because they have nothing else better to do – no specialist interests – nothing! Realize, too, that work for them is primarily a social function. They go to work first to socialize, then to do the job, then to get paid. Without the socialization aspect of the job, NTs would be even more unhappy in their place of work. The upshot of this is you must be prepared to put up with unintelligible, mundane banalities that most NTs pass off as communication. You must be prepared to take part in all the little nonsense social games they like to play, like winding people up all the time. You must be able to put up with a world of small-minded priorities that are purely peer driven. NTs don't do anything without the approval of the people around them...not that you would get any them of to admit to such a shallow thing! They do not like to stand out.

Next important thing is: the NT workplace is all about the popularity contest. The ability to prove over and over again that your ego is the biggest and the best – the best at fitting in. If you are male, you will be required to take part in the metaphorical 'dick-measuring' contest, and be able to talk fluently about sports, beer and sex. So just be aware of this environment that prevails and pervades mainstream society. Be aware that life has been built by and suffers badly from a condition called NTBD – Neurotypical Blerk Disorder – and I'm afraid to say...there is no known cure for it at the moment. The main components of this condition are:

1. Mr Blerk knows best.

2. Mr Blerk's decision is final.

3.   Mr Blerk always thinks he's in charge.

If you are female, then compulsory reading of every aspirational magazine like *Hello, Heat, Chat* etc., is required. So then you will be able to take part in irrelevant discussions about what the rich and famous may or may not be doing, and also holidays, kids and of course – Blerks. Personally, I can't think of anything more abhorrent – no wonder the AS suicide rate stands at six per cent higher than the national average…and we're expected to fit in with this?

Talking about fitting in…do not ever forget that NTs are naturally xenophobic. You only have to look at their historic attitudes towards black people, gays, transsexuals, people with religious differences and the disabled to understand that these so-called 'nice' people are not so nice after all. Especially when their nonsensical sensibilities and their social taboos are being threatened. We wouldn't need a Hate Crime and Diversity Division in the police force otherwise. They are afraid of anything different. They deal with difference by blaming it on the person with the difference, by passing it off as a 'life choice', implying that I choose to be different. A quote I came across the other day goes: 'What is the point of being healthily adjusted to a sick society?'…just something for you to think about before you decide to contribute to the mainstream at large.

My view on all of this is…if I am going to make any contribution at all, then it will be to the AS community…my own people, my own genotype…where I naturally belong.

The only direction that I've found in the way of integrating in any vocational way, is to work to my Aspergian strengths, and I suppose could be seen as an alternative route to employment if that's the road you want to go down. But it has worked very well for me.

Once I became aware of the plight of Aspergians in mainstream society, it got my back up. This was a cause I could not help but feel strongly about, and for me, this was what I'd been searching for all my life. It appealed to my innate and very sensitive sense of justice and fair play – none of which I'd experienced much of in dealing with the NT world. Once I'd got my diagnosis in 2003, doors opened that had been firmly shut.

Aspergians are great at taking up causes. The fight for rights comes naturally to us, and for those who can, we will be seen right at the front fighting injustice and the bullies and lies – it's what we are, it's what we do.

Luckily I ended up volunteering for our local autistic charity – luckily because it's right on my doorstep. Action for ASD is mainly for children and adolescents, dealing in the main with Asperger Syndrome. At some time in the future, I hope, there will be funding for adults. It still amazes me that the majority of NTs are amazed that autistic children grow up into autistic adults – where the hell do they think we go?

Luckily we have an Asperger-specific counsellor. Luckily there are people working there who know and understand the Aspergian world, and yes amazingly they are neurotypical. The environment is Asperger friendly, where I can be as eccentric as I like and not get judged unfavourably. It means I can live within the Aspergian 'envelope', it means I can bypass the NT world, it means that I can engage in my specialist interest, which is Asperger Syndrome.

This works for me in the following ways:

> I need autonomy, this means I can be in control at all times, this means I can control the amount of pressure I'm put under.

> I work with people who are aware of and understand Aspergian expectations, and who do not impose NT expectations on myself.

> The building is sympathetic, as are the staff, to my sensory requirements, which are many: visual, auditory, tactile and olfactory.

> Because of my extensive AS knowledge, I am in a position to train and educate a wide variety of people about the unique world of the Aspergian, giving specific training days, as well as my personal perspective of what its like to live with Asperger's.

> So this gives me momentum, purpose and direction – it plays to my Aspergian strengths – I can freely promote the Aspergian cause.

> The number of people I work with is small. So this cuts down on overload – very important.

> I mentor other Aspergians on how to be Aspergian, how to be proud of the unique gift it can be if allowed to flourish. This I can do by drawing on my outside world experiences, and how I have, and haven't coped within an unsympathetic society.

To work within an NT environment means educating the people whom you work with to a very high degree and understanding of Asperger

Syndrome. There are many good publications out there that cover this. Getting these people to undertake this homework is another thing entirely. All I can say is good luck on that one, but you will be up against belligerence and arrogance and intolerance.

Working inside Aspergian expectations, in a purely Aspergian way, has lifted the misery of dealing with people who wouldn't normally accept me as I am. It gives me the long-sighted opportunity of working towards an individual Aspergian society, where Asperger Syndrome would be celebrated, where this neurological difference would be allowed to reach its full potential, where everyone – ASs and NTs alike – could be accepted for who and what they are.

Remember – it's not that you are not ready for society – society isn't ready for you.

Thank you for indulging me,

Cornish

Chapter 11: A Melmacian in the Workplace: Asperger Syndrome for Employers

Chris Mitchell

Introduction by Luke Beardon

Chris's excellent advice in this chapter should be read by all employers or potential employers – i.e. everyone! It's refreshing to see that the writing is aimed at the employer rather than the employee – I hope to get across the message that change should lie just as much with the employer as with the person with AS. For each individual, support and adaptations are going to be different. It is helpful to break everything down into categories to ensure that support is as individual as possible. For example, categories might include:

- *communication style*
- *social needs*
- *organizational abilities*
- *anxiety levels*
- *sensory issues*
- *abilities in understanding what to do*
- *timing.*

This is not an exhaustive list – but for each of the above the employer needs to have a good understanding of what impact each category has for the individual in order to make sure appropriate support is in place for each one. For example, communication abilities need careful assessment. Ask questions such as: what is the preferred mode of communication, receptively and expressively? Is there a problem with ambiguous language? What level of precision in language is needed? Do there need to be clear boundaries around what is acceptable language to use and what is not? Does the individual enjoy social communication or not? Are there clear rules for when, where and with whom to communicate within the workplace? Is there a clear pathway for the individual to take if communication is not understood? Again, this is not an exhaustive list, but for each of the categories above these are the sorts of questions that need to be asked in order for an appropriate assessment to be made before the employer can begin to understand what adjustments and support are required.

Despite increasing awareness of Asperger Syndrome, the percentage of people diagnosed with Asperger Syndrome in full-time employment remains low. Equally of concern is the difficulty many people with Asperger Syndrome who have been able to obtain employment have to maintain it. This chapter looks at potential strategies for potential employers to help develop good relations with an Asperger Syndrome employee, get the best out of the Asperger Syndrome employee and, above all to help realize that many people diagnosed with Asperger Syndrome can make very effective employees if given the right training and encouragement.

Benefits of a diagnosis and disclosure

As many people with Asperger Syndrome have experienced low self-esteem, social isolation and general lack of understanding among others, it can be very easy to feel that being diagnosed with Asperger Syndrome can mean being excluded from access to employment. But this should not be the case. If anything, a diagnosis of Asperger Syndrome can be of great benefit, not just in terms of being able to access employment, but also in helping the individual with Asperger Syndrome identify their strengths and weaknesses. This way, they can decide, together with careers advisors and potential employers, suitable positions where their strengths can be used effectively as well as unsuitable positions to keep away from where their weaknesses may be exposed.

This aspect of the procedure of applying for and obtaining jobs often presents a 'Catch 22' situation to many potential employees with Asperger Syndrome, whether or not to disclose their diagnosis. The author of this chapter at first didn't feel it necessary to disclose his Asperger Syndrome diagnosis when first applying for jobs, but when a difficulty arose in the working environment, the supervisor and colleagues were unable to understand the source of the problem.

Since this experience, the author strongly recommends disclosure of an Asperger Syndrome diagnosis, so that potential employers can be informed of any potential misunderstandings they may otherwise experience and most importantly, so that they can't discriminate against it. In accordance with the Disability Discrimination Act 1995, if a job applicant with a disability (including Asperger Syndrome) meets the essential criteria for the post, the employer is obliged to invite the candidate to an interview, particularly if they have the 'Positive About Disabled People' quality mark.

Barriers to the job market

There are many people with Asperger Syndrome, who are no different to other candidates in terms of their skills and qualifications. It can often be the case where an NT candidate and an Asperger Syndrome candidate can present almost identical resumés on paper. However, where the difference is often likely to emerge is at the interview stage and during the procedure of networking, including difficulty developing social relations with potential employers. It is often frustrating for many potential employees in that they feel unable to access the jobs market appropriate to their skills/qualifications due to difficulties with the social skills often required in obtaining employment.

Understanding among potential employers can also be a barrier, especially if they interpret Asperger Syndrome as something that it is not. Potential employers feel 'threatened' by a potential employee with Asperger Syndrome appearing different. There has even been an occasion when a potential employee with Asperger Syndrome was turned down for a job on the grounds that 'they may have a fit and kill somebody' (Beaumont 2001).

Being able to obtain employment is one major barrier for many people with Asperger Syndrome, but perhaps an even greater barrier can often be maintaining a job. To feel secure and generally happy in a job, it often helps to develop good social relations with work colleagues. An employee with

Asperger Syndrome, however, may prefer to keep to themselves, not understanding the unwritten rules of being able to develop such good working relations, including being able to relate to workplace topics of conversation. This way, they can appear as a target for isolation, or in some cases even harassment.

Issues in the Workplace
WORKPLACE HIERARCHY AND LANGUAGE
An employee with Asperger Syndrome is often blind to unwritten rules of social interaction, and in a working environment, they may not immediately recognize the often invisible workplace hierarchy, including to whom they are accountable themselves, and to whom their respective line manager is accountable.

Workplace hierarchies vary dramatically between organizations, and may be more or less fragmented depending on the nature of the organization. Sometimes, the more fragmented a workplace hierarchy, the more confusing it can be for an Asperger Syndrome employee. Sadly, inability to grasp workplace hierarchies can sometimes be mistaken for ignorance.

The language and social cues used in the working environment may also be difficult for an employee with Asperger Syndrome to grasp, including the workings of staff/team meetings. The Asperger Syndrome employee may often want to put across a discussion point or idea in such a situation, but may have difficulty in recognizing when to speak, and may unintentionally interrupt. Again, this can be mistaken for rudeness.

Dress codes can also be confusing sometimes, particularly in a role that involves a high degree of variation within tasks. For instance, many clerical/office jobs may involve a degree of filing or office/store-room tidying, for which office-associated smart dress codes may not be appropriate. In other roles, it may not be apparent to an Asperger Syndrome employee as to why it is necessary to dress smartly. For instance, working in a call centre, smart dress codes may not appear necessary as a call-centre operator deals with customers verbally rather than face to face. However, in some call centres it may be that clients can visit the site at any time, so a smart image is perhaps desirable.

ANXIETY
Other issues within a working environment may cause high levels of anxiety for an employee with Asperger Syndrome. Roles that run off one's

own time management, where there is a lunch break or start/finish time can cause anxiety for an employee with Asperger Syndrome, in the sense that the role can be unpredictable and it can become very difficult to anticipate what may occur that can change the direction of their output. The author of this work felt a constant need to keep taking 'short snacks' of crisps and biscuits when working as an academic research assistant, a role run purely off the employee's own time management. This way one may experience eating disorders through not eating balanced meals.

In some organizations, there may be a culture of competitiveness between employees. Though some interpretations of Asperger Syndrome suggest that people with the condition prefer to work on their own, others with Asperger Syndrome may not feel comfortable working within an environment where everyone is competing against one another, as this can cause much stress and anxiety. In organizations such as the media (e.g. newspaper, advertising industries etc.) or insurance/sales services, individual employees often have their own agenda, and may be competing against one another to hit targets, extract commission or achieve promotion. This may often be at the expense of others and, as a result, can create conflict, thus leading to further anxiety in an employee with Asperger Syndrome.

Such anxiety in an employee with Asperger Syndrome can also be linked to their job security, particularly in roles that are temporary or contract-based. Though the issue of job security in such roles applies to non-Asperger Syndrome employees, the quality of the work/output of an employee with Asperger Syndrome who experiences difficulty in being able to manage high levels of anxiety can suffer.

ISSUES IN TRAINING

An employee with Asperger Syndrome's ability to focus and absorb training may be different to others' when learning a new job or incorporating a new task into their current role. When trying to absorb training being conducted, an employee with Asperger Syndrome may be very 'one-channel' in their ability to focus, often struggling to see where different elements of training fit into the process as a whole.

Such inabilities can unfortunately be mistaken for the Asperger Syndrome employee not paying attention, and the employee with Asperger Syndrome may feel that too much is expected of them. In the long run, this can mean continued frustration for the employer and excessive pressure for the Asperger Syndrome employee.

The author of this chapter, incidentally, believes that people with Asperger Syndrome can make good trainers/managers as they are often least likely to expect those they are training to master skills quickly, particularly if they have struggled with them themselves. This approach takes away pressure on those learning a new skill making it much easier to learn.

Potential solutions

OBTAINING EMPLOYMENT
Some suggestions to help identify and obtain a suitable position for an employee with Asperger Syndrome include:

- To give an Asperger Syndrome candidate a fair chance at interview, it may be helpful to let the candidate view the interview questions before the actual interview, so that they can structure appropriate answers, rather than having to struggle to collect their thoughts under pressure.

- To identify a suitable position for an employee, an aptitude test may be beneficial. This can also help identify the candidate's strengths/skills so they can be put to good use.

- Employers could discuss with the candidate any necessary arrangements to enable the candidate to perform their job better (e.g. a workspace not too close to colleagues).

- So that the candidate can get used to their place of work and their employer, a probationary/trial period may help. This would also help the candidate find out if a role is suitable or unsuitable for them.

MAINTAINING EMPLOYMENT
To help an employee with Asperger Syndrome keep employment and generally feel secure, some suggestions include:

- Potential employers could be informed about Asperger Syndrome and the difficulties the Asperger Syndrome employee may experience.

- To avoid anxiety, a timetabled routine with clear start and finish times and lunch break would be beneficial.

- A 'buddy system' could be employed to avoid isolation and potential harassment/conflict. Access to a support worker would also be beneficial.

- On-the-job training can be beneficial, as the Asperger Syndrome employee may have difficulty applying college-based training to the workplace.

TRAINING

Issues in training for employers to take note of when training an employee with Asperger Syndrome include:

- Don't expect an employee with Asperger Syndrome to master skills as quickly as others.

- Don't expect them to multi-task easily, as the Asperger Syndrome employee may have difficulty transferring skills from one area to another.

Some potentially Asperger-friendly training methods include:

- *Use 'chunk' information* – Break the job down into simple tasks, explaining each part, before showing how all tasks demonstrated link in with one another. Visual aids to show links can also be useful.

- *Acting out tasks* – Acting out how to do different tasks within a job can help the person learn (e.g. franking mail, talking to customers etc.).

- *Repeat tasks* – Encourage the employee to repeat tasks once they have learned them, so they will become second nature.

- *Give positive feedback* – Including helping the employee recognize mistakes where necessary.

Bibliography

Beaumont, P. (2001) 'Adult victims of autism are left on jobs scrapheap' *The Observer*, 13 May.

Chapter 12: Surviving the Workplace: Asperger Syndrome at Work

Stuart Vallantine

Introduction by Luke Beardon

Stuart demonstrates one of the strongest characteristics that so many individuals with AS have – that of having higher levels of determination than their NT counterparts. As with most characteristics of AS this is yet another example of why a person with AS should theoretically make for a good employee. It is unfortunate to say the least that the social side of things so often gets in the way of work, but since the social side of things tends to be the domain of the NTs, it would seem sensible to suggest that the problems are NT problems, not related to the working practice itself. This may seem a naive perspective, and I am not for one minute suggesting that it is as easy as all that, but certainly more social acceptance of how people with AS are rather than punishing them for who they are would be a step in the right direction.

The interview or assessment test worked out well for you, and some time later, the company contacts you by post or telephone with those words, 'You've got the job'. After overcoming this, you are either pleased or indifferent to the whole thing.

Sometimes you may be nervous at travelling to work seven minutes or seven miles away from home. You wonder whether you would get on with your fellow colleagues or not. Or you wonder if you would wake up in time for the bus.

From personal experience, it took me eight years to gain the position which most suited my abilities. My previous positions were temporary jobs, subsidized by the UK Government's New Deal scheme. Prior to that, I spent two years on a Youth Training scheme. During this time, I also spent five years in college, part-time and voluntary positions. In the latter part of 2002, I had a telephone call stating my success in gaining the position. After numerous interviews in the last year alone, this came as a surprise. I landed the position after one interview and two assessment tests.

In getting my first unsubsidized job, I was able to get used to the idea of travelling to and from work, arriving on time and looking smart enough for the job. Then I found there were other 'rules', where 'going to work' meant more than clocking on or off and getting the job done professionally. For the most part, this meant peer relationships (for example, post-work drinks with fellow colleagues), other social rules (respecting one's privacy if someone is phoning a customer or family member) and flexibility (if important jobs require immediate deadlines).

For the purpose of this section, I shall incorporate references of my current experience with recommendations for settling down at work and holding down a job. This will include references to starting work, settling in and interacting with fellow colleagues in the work environment. Most references to my personal experience pertain to working in administrative and technical positions I have held in the last ten years.

Preparing for work

My first unsubsidized position in January 2003 was a welcome relief from nearly 18 months of signing on. I had found the obligation of finding a given number of jobs arduous and in some parts unrewarding. This was in spite of numerous interviews, two weeks at an interview skills workshop and experience through voluntary work. What kept me through those lean times were dogged persistence and self-belief. For a period where I wasn't obliged to participate in job searching, I still checked the local newspapers – having had that earlier routine entrenched from my first year of unemployment. I did so in the hope my dream position was buried somewhere within the jobs section – or on the local Job Centre's computerized displays.

TRANSITION TO WORK

Almost as soon as you start your new job, sufficient notice must be given by the employee or previous employer. If you are moving to a new position from your previous company, sufficient notice of approach would be given by the previous employer. Typically, this would be for one calendar month.

If on State benefits, such as the Disability Living Allowance, or Jobseekers' Allowance, you are required to inform your nearest Job Centre of the start date of your new position. From my experience, I contacted my local Job Centre, and was issued a 'signing-off' form. This form requires you to fill in details of your new job, including contact details and the start date. On completion, the form is returned to the Job Centre in person, or by post. Your Jobseekers' Allowance claim is terminated from the date you start work. If the position you are in is a temporary job, your records are retained, which saves you from making a new claim.

TRANSPORT

If possible, it would be worth making the journey to your prospective workplace before you start working there. Doing this will avoid any slip-ups on the first day of starting work. It may be worth making the journey to your prospective workplace during the rush hour. This will give you a better idea of the journey time than one made on a Sunday afternoon.

Whilst in the proximity of your prospective office block, industrial unit or building site, use the journey to investigate parking facilities, bus and tram stops or railway stations. Though most of the homework may have been done on the day of the interview, it is worth researching this further. This is especially true if you are unfamiliar with the area.

Before starting work, assess the nearest or cheapest car parking facilities, or pick up the appropriate timetable(s) from your nearest bus information office, tourist information centre or railway ticket office. In some areas, timetables are available in local libraries, newsagents and health centres. If you are unable to do this, some timetables are available by post from local authorities or transport operators, or via internet sites such as

Transport Direct or National Rail. Most transport companies include time-table information and route maps via their websites.

Some companies may offer staff car parking facilities. Otherwise, if your line of work is within an urban area, where parking is at a premium, find a car park within short walking distance of the premises.

If using public transport, I would recommend choosing the journey which would get you to work within 30 minutes of the start time rather than within 30 seconds. From past experience, I have realized this issue; in some instances, I had had ten minutes to go till starting work, resulting in me making a spirited dash to the office, looking flustered – thus having an effect on my performance at work.

For using public transport, I recommend:

- planning several ways of travelling to work, if you are lucky enough to live in an area with a wide range of journey options

- opting for the quickest possible route, or one with the fewest changes of bus, train, tram or underground train

- choosing a route which is less likely to suffer from traffic congestion or overcrowding

- carrying a copy, or copies of the latest timetable(s).

Prior to starting work, I recommend researching the parking rates and public transport fares. If your workplace is close to pay-and-display car parks, find one which is the closest, the cheapest and the most secure, ideally one within 15 minutes' walk away. Company parking spaces may be designated to senior members of staff, require a permit or be free to all employees.

When travelling on public transport, it may be worth checking the operator's website or ringing their offices, when requesting information on single or return fares. Usually, the operator's number is printed in time-tables. Alternatively, enquiries may be made at staffed railway stations or transport information centres.

If you are making more than two journeys a day, it may be worthwhile purchasing a season ticket. Not only would this pay for your journeys to and from work, it would also pay for journeys made outside work for leisure use.

CLOTHES

On this same preliminary journey, you could consider buying appropriate clothing for the job prior to starting. If the starting date of your position is some time away (for example a month off), consider buying online or going to the shops at less busy times. If you have existing clothes from a similar position, make the best use of these. For the first few weeks, you could borrow your fellow relatives' clothes (I spent the first few days in work borrowing my father's shirts and ties before being able to afford my own).

For clerical and technical positions, businesses favour smart dress and sober colours. Skirts should be kept to reasonable length, ideally below the knee, ties should ideally be plain or neatly patterned and shoes should be smart and comfortable. The Mickey Mouse tie you wore at a relative's Christmas do may win you brief popularity with your immediate col-leagues, but not the boss or line manager. Your choice of footwear should be comfortable enough for over eight hours of continuous wear a day.

Sometimes, the need to shop around for clothes is eliminated in most part by company uniforms. In most cases, parts of the company's uniform are available free to employees, with the employee being obliged to purchase the remainder of their uniform. This has some advantages, in that one half of the clothing has been sorted out. One disadvantage is the person wearing one part of the clothing, supplied by the company, may feel disorientated by the materials. For example, the collar of the polo shirt may be claustrophobic on the neck, or the sleeves may be too tight. I have a similar issue with my own work shirts, resulting in me wearing shirts more suited to a sumo wrestler, due to the tightness around the collar.

As well as looking smart or comfortable (depending on the line of work), members of staff may be fed up with seeing you in the same clothes day in, day out.

Things to consider:

- skirts at reasonable, below the knee, length
- ties with plain colours or sensible pattern designs
- comfortable though formal shoes (office environments).

FOOD

Prior to starting your new job, it may be a good idea to evaluate possible sandwich shops, supermarkets and cafés within a short distance from your workplace. This may save you time wandering around during the lunch break.

The best idea, in terms of minimal expense, is to take a packed lunch. If, for example, you have a gluten and/or casein intolerance, a packed lunch is a must. To avoid rushing around on the first day you start work, preparing your packed lunch the night before is a worthwhile idea. This is especially true if the workplace is miles away from a café or sandwich shop, let alone a health food shop or supermarket selling GF/CF products.

Prior to starting my current position, I had few problems in preparing for the first day, having almost as good as spent eight years doing that, in between temporary jobs and voluntary work. I was lucky to have a long preparation period between finding out about my success and actually starting my job. Thankfully, I had enough clothes to keep me going for the first month before I received my first monthly salary, most of which came via my father and from previous job interviews.

I was also fortunate enough to find a position in a familiar area, though diligently planned my journeys to allow for peak period traffic. Some time before I started, I realized the need not only to be in work on time, but also to allow sufficient time for changes in traffic conditions. I have found being in work early an antidote to rushing from bus or train to the office.

Your first day at work
Things to remember:

- P45
- packed lunch
- transport pass or loose change for bus, train, tram or underground rail system(s)
- bank details.

On the first day of work, the most important things to remember are your bank details and tax details. In the United Kingdom, the form displaying your tax details is a P45. This form is retained by the employer of your present position and is returned to you after you finish your previous job.

For your first day at work, it may be worthwhile to take a packed lunch rather than look around for sandwich shops or supermarkets. Sometimes, your fellow colleagues will recommend their favoured sandwich shop or similar food outlet. If your company premises are miles away from such outlets, a packed lunch may be the only option, unless mobile sandwich shops are available.

For your first day, consider buying a day saver ticket or a return ticket. In some cases, the former is cheaper than two single fares, or one return fare. If your place of work is a short journey (for example, less than ten minutes away from home by bus), on a direct bus route, two single fares or a return ticket may work out cheaper than a day saver.

If you are a regular public transport user, it may be worth purchasing a season ticket for your favoured mode(s) of transport to and from work. If you make most of your journeys using one company's transport routes, it may be worth buying a season ticket for that one company's routes. Alternatively, if your route has more than one operator, it may be possible in some areas to purchase season tickets covering all companies within your locality. Some can be bought on the bus, train or trams, automatic ticket machines or ticket offices and transport information centres.

I, for the first month of starting work, bought a weekly ticket from the company whose buses I most used, and purchased a day saver ticket or a single fare for non-essential travel for routes outside my favoured operator's territory.

On starting your new job, your bank details are equally as important as your P45. Required information includes the bank's sort code (displayed as six numbers twice hyphenated to denote your branch details) and your account number. This is important, as companies are unable to pay your wages as cash in hand or in cheque form, and therefore pay them directly into your bank account. Most companies pay wages by the calendar month on a set date, at which time they are credited to your bank account.

Settling in

I found myself most settled after my third week into my first subsidized job. By then, I had to learn a new set of rules, and learn to get on with other colleagues. This also meant adjusting to a nine-to-five weekday pattern and coping with the worst excesses of rush-hour traffic.

Some companies may provide you with a company handbook, stating the rules of working with their company. Another source is your contract of employment, which in writing states your roles and responsibilities. This is handed to all employees, within the first week of joining. A copy of this could be made for personal reference, with the original copy left with the employer.

All UK-based companies are also governed by another set of rules: the 1974 Health and Safety at Work Act. This encourages safe systems of working practices and is enforced by a Government body, the Health and Safety Executive.

The most obvious routine of all is your working hours, such as which times for the lunch break or coffee breaks. Some companies insist on set times for all employees, though lunch rotas are now a more popular option. For instance, a company in a sales-led environment would insist on a rota system, so as to keep the telephones manned all day. In this instance, Person A may have their lunch at 12.30 p.m., with Person B taking lunch 30 minutes later. Assuming the company offers a 30-minute lunch break, this arrangement would maintain continuity for their sales department or help desk.

I have always found eating my lunch away from the workplace preferable to eating at the desk. This gives me the idea that I am on my lunch break and am therefore less distracted from my job, returning refreshed. I have found eating lunch at my desk a distraction, thus diminishing the value of my lunch hour. On these grounds, I recommend having your lunch away from your workplace, or in a different room.

Increasingly, businesses have adopted shift patterns as opposed to the standard nine-to-five, five-days-a-week working hours. In most industrialized countries, service industries have led to more flexible working hours and options for part-time work. According the European Union's Working Time Directive, employees within EU countries can work up to 48 hours a week (equal to eight hours a day, six days a week). There is also an opt-out clause, where persons can sign to work beyond the statutory 48 hours a week. The UK is the only EU member state which offers this clause.

As per the EU Working Time Directive, citizens within the European Union are entitled to a minimum of four weeks' paid holidays – plus national bank holidays. Some outside the EU are entitled to fewer than the four weeks.

It is commonplace for most companies to allocate holiday arrangements on a first come, first served basis, to ensure that the office or production line has adequate cover. In most cases, two individuals at the most could take time off at the same time.

I recommend booking longer periods of time off as early as possible to avoid disappointment. In most cases, companies will expect a longer period of notice (for example, one month) for employees taking five or more days off from work, than one booking half a day off. The longer period of notice allows companies to arrange cover for that period, by either re-allocating work to other employees or taking on a temporary employee, and sufficient notice is given for the company's pay roll bureau. For individual days off, I, too, recommend booking early, at least two weeks' minimum notice – especially if that day's of great importance to you (for example, your birthday or other special event).

Some companies only offer one period for employees to book their holidays by closing down for a week or two at periods where production would be at its lowest. This is a very rare practice, inherited from heavy industries and manufacturing companies.

Underpinning this is your contract of employment. This is a legally binding document signed by yourself and the supervisor. Incorporated within this document are your holiday entitlement details, working hours, roles and responsibilities, and company rules. In some cases, you may be required to work unpaid overtime. Sometimes, this may mean working odd hours for free, usually to finish off urgent projects. If, for example, a certain project was subject to a strict deadline, employees would work an extra few hours to finish the project on time. This is especially so in salaried positions.

For permanent or fixed-term contract jobs, most companies offer a set probationary period, where the employee is given, for example, six weeks to prove themselves. In some cases, holiday entitlement may be unavailable for that probationary period. The successful employee's job would be made permanent thereafter. In the case of short-term temporary jobs, holiday entitlements may be unavailable.

Getting paid

In most cases, staff are paid on a monthly basis on any given date of the calendar month. This can take the form of a certain day in the month, or any part of the week or month. Staff are usually paid a fixed salary per year, or pay information is derived from the employee's clock card or time sheet.

A clock card is given to employees on joining the company, and displays details of the times that they arrived at or left work. Staff are paid for the exact times they were present by inserting their clock card into a clocking machine. The clocking machine will stamp the actual date and time onto the card.

A time sheet is similar to this, though often on paper or computerized form. The employee fills the hours in which they worked. This is signed by both the employee and their supervisor.

On receiving your pay slip, the pay slip will display details of deductions for income tax and National Insurance or Social Security contributions. In England and Wales, Student Loan deductions may also be made on graduates earning £15,000 per year (2007 figures) or above. By the end of March, UK-based employees receive a P60, in addition to their pay slips. This details the amount of income tax and National Insurance contributions, over the period from the first day in April of the year to the last day in March of the following year. This P60 is retained by the employee.

On starting work, it is common for employees to work what is referred to as a 'week in hand' or a 'month in hand'. This is the most difficult part of starting work. In most cases, you would for your first few days or weeks at work be paid that rate rather than a full month's pay. This means, for instance, stretching your first week's pay over a calendar month, and not receiving your full month's pay till the end of the second month of employment.

Harder still – and especially true for the first month of being in work – is budgeting with the remainder of your previous salary or state benefits. One thing I strongly recommend doing is drawing up a budget of your weekly outgoings. This should include expenditure on travel to and from work, food and drink. As stated earlier, I recommend taking a packed lunch for your first month in work. This is a more cost-effective idea than using the nearest sandwich shop or fast food outlet. On receiving your first full monthly salary, I recommend revising your budget to allow for increased outgoings, such as travel, food and any outstanding payments, and disposable income.

Getting down to work
STRUCTURE

In work situations, I have considered myself a hard-working person – a hard-working person if everything seems to be going my way. If for example, the computer crashed, I along with several other people would be annoyed by this. However, this annoyance would be too much of a distraction, resulting in me thinking 'where was I?' or wandering off course. Sometimes I could be too chatty to the ire of other colleagues. At the other end of the scale, I could be totally engrossed in something and forget everything else.

People with Asperger Syndrome and similar autism spectrum disorders may be seen by some as single minded, a description which may be seen both ways. In the positive sense, this means devotion to their work. In another sense, this may be seen as having knowledge in a limited area and the perception that 'Person X knows everything about Linux operating systems and nothing else'. In my case, this means being able to do a task and see it to the finish – sometimes at the expense of other assignments. Some may also be goal orientated and be able to meet or exceed targets.

I've always found a well-structured day best suited to my needs, though not to the point where each day would be too repetitive. A good idea would be a timetable or a 'to do' chart. One of these could be helpful in prioritizing one's workload. This could take the form of a wipe clean board or a standard exercise book. I would recommend splitting the chart into these categories: immediate (for tasks which require completion on the same day), ongoing (low-priority ongoing tasks, i.e. general administrative tasks including photocopying duties) and main tasks. This could include separate columns for the proposed completion date of each task. Alternatively, a diary (especially one in a 'Page a Day' format) would suffice. A timetable constructed using a spreadsheet program is equally helpful. This has the bonus of not cluttering the desk or working area the same.

SENSORY ISSUES

Having a sense of structure gives me a degree of certainty, and is the difference between me wandering off track or concentrating on my task efficiently. However, I can also be distracted by sensory issues, such as telephones ringing, background noise from conversations and the fire alarm. Whilst at school, I was upset by the noise of the fire bell. Even to this day I am still shaken by the noise of the fire alarm, with my current place of employment having weekly fire drills at set times. At this point, I am distracted from work activities, even with earplugs.

I always wear my earplugs during the fire drill, and sometimes wear them when background noise at work goes beyond a comfortable volume.

If the background noise from conversations and chatting is affecting me, I feel as though I'm drowning and shutting off, like a computer on the verge of crashing.

Another issue I've had is lighting. I tend to work better if natural light is well balanced with artificial light. In previous buildings I have worked in, I have found working under fluorescent lighting a nightmare. This has been more pronounced on dull days and late afternoons between late October and late March in the following year. Sometimes, if the contrast was too high for me, I would rest my eyes for a few seconds or a few minutes. Even when I was wearing glasses with anti-reflective lenses, I would still get the same effect, though less pronounced.

If the lighting is too much, I would recommend a pair of cheap sunglasses. If you have tinted lenses, such as Irlen lenses or any similar make, I would recommend making the most of these. For aural sensory issues, a cheap pair of earplugs would suffice. To shut out background noise, some employers may allow you to work with your personal stereo or MP3 player.

Another idea I recommend is being able to take a few minutes away from your desk or machine. If that is possible, I recommend asking your supervisor if you could take a few minutes away from the desk or machine. This could take the form of a short walk near your workplace, or by asking fellow colleagues if they would fancy a drink of tea or coffee (unless the company has set break times). For your 'time out' session, concentrate on something which is less likely to overload you.

Peer relationships

In my current job, I have had fewer problems working with people in my line of work compared with my earlier years in mainstream education. Luckily, most of my colleagues have accepted me for what I am rather than the fact I have an autism spectrum disorder. This has led to me raising awareness of Semantic Pragmatic Language Disorder and Asperger Syndrome. This took me the best part of six to nine months, and I have had fewer problems since.

It wasn't always that smooth in my previous temporary jobs and Youth Training. In the latter case, messing about from other colleagues distracted me to the point I was upset – and this continued till my training provider moved to the other end of the town to a college. In my first temporary job, this improved, due to the wider mix of persons and age ranges making for a relaxed atmosphere.

POST-WORK

In the last few years, I have found good peer relationships as essential to surviving in the workplace as producing work to a high standard. In this period, I have found how important it is to get on with your colleagues without losing 'me' in the process. My experience has proved that going to the pub after work is not 'compulsory', in order to interact with fellow colleagues. If the pub is one where the noise is akin to a jumbo jet in take-off, I avoid it or take a pair of earplugs. In such places, I was happy if the noisy pub had music blaring away rather than the noise of conversation. If the conversation was too deafening, I would turn my attention to the background noise, or find some spare change for the jukebox.

Some may regard saying 'no' to the post-work pint as impolite. Others may be more forgiving and understand that Person X may need to catch their bus home. I have often pulled out of post-work drinking sessions either with the simple excuse of needing the bus home – or preferring a quieter pub nearer home. If the person's choice of pub is too noisy, I would kindly refuse the offer. This would be based on previous visits, if I had found the place too noisy.

No one is obliged to stay in the pub till closing time for a post-work drink. I have always said, 'I'll just go have one [pint] and go home'. Colleagues may be as satisfied if one of their fellows goes for one pint as for ten, since the favour and invitation has been returned and accepted. My other reason for drinking sensibly has been the loss of control over myself after a certain amount of pints or units, and myself being ineffectual and awkward.

If a drink after work is not your idea of relaxation, you could politely refuse by stating you need to catch the bus or train home or that you are driving. Alternatively, you could state the fact you have an important appointment or children to look after. The post-work meeting-place doesn't have to be their chosen pub. Instead, it could be caffeine over alcohol, in a local coffee house. Or it could be a familiar café, fast-food outlet or quieter pub.

AT WORK

One thing I have found is that getting on with your colleagues is not the subject of a popularity contest. In time, I have earned respect by being knowledgeable about my line of work and providing straight advice in my professional capacity. Having worked in my current position for some time, some have noticed how I've adjusted well to the work environment. However, I do find some aspects difficult.

Sometimes I've been indiscreet, and at other times I have been less than forthcoming in asking for help. My reason has been fear of being indiscreet and disrupting a colleague from their task. It may be worthwhile approaching the person you wish to speak to in an indirectly confrontational way. In this way, I recommend using a post-it note and placing it on the person's desk. I find this method preferable to email, due to the time involved in composing a message in this format. This is especially true if the person is in the middle of a phone call.

COPING WITH CHANGE

If any changes are made to my job or to an aspect of day-to-day living I appreciate being given sufficient notice to prepare in advance. In the last four years, through expansion, my current employer has made four moves, though within the same city. The move from one office or factory to another is stressful for all companies and their employees. At one end of the scale, this means changes in travel plans and moving to a strange town. At the other end, this means ensuring the transfer from Building A to Building B was effective enough for the business concerned.

In my current position, I have been informed well in advance of any moves or changes in role. I was informed a month before these transfers were effective, along with my other colleagues. During my Youth Training period, I was informed of the move from a more work-based environment to a more college-based environment a month in advance. This was following the transfer of my Youth Training scheme provider to that of a local college, which I found more suitable.

BULLYING AND HARASSMENT

From my experience, I have found bullying at work to be more subtle than the playground variety. It could take the form of harassment by email, the low-tech approach of being shown up in front of fellow workers, or being lumbered with the most demeaning tasks. At present, I have had no issues regarding harassment at work. My colleagues have understood 'me' and valued rather than ridiculed my differences.

A few years ago, this wasn't the case. I experienced some verbal harassment from a colleague, reducing me to tears. A fellow employee told me that the person was picking on me. I didn't think at the time that the person was bullying me. I thought that was part of working life and surviving the workplace. One incident almost reduced me to tears, and at that point I shouted 'I'm gonna do one'. When I headed towards the exit, another colleague came to me and my stay away from the office was less than five minutes. More of the same happened the following day. I broke down in tears, retired to the toilets and found the protagonist in the lavatory apologizing – despite myself still being in tears. I was allowed a longer lunch break, finding sanctuary in a nearby art gallery.

Closer to the playground variety was the bullying I experienced in Youth Training. With most of my fellows fresh from leaving school, bullying was more the verbal variety, or that of moving a person's equipment to an unknown (to the person targeted) part of the office or workshop. I joined hoping to get hands-on experience and a qualification, with the lure of day release at a local college. Most of the bullying involved the removal of pens or pencils which upset me. Once more, I thought tolerating this was part of surviving a Youth Training scheme.

Until recently, I was often afraid of reporting such incidents, on account of previous experience. Sometimes, it has been my fear of somebody repeating Aesop's fable on crying wolf. However, if you feel that someone has harassed you, speak out.

Placed within your information pack or company handbook is the company's grievance policy, with the required information for reporting incidents, bullying or harassment from fellow members of staff. If you feel a bit nervous about speaking to your supervisor, an email or letter is a good alternative. This is best written during lunch break or outside work hours. If you feel the need to speak to the supervisor directly, I would recommend asking if you could speak to them in a separate room. If you intend to have a short meeting (five minutes or less), you could give them notice the same day. For lengthier meetings (over five minutes), I would recommend stating your reasons for the meeting and asking the supervisor which day they are available. It may be more polite to give at least two days' notice, which allows time for them to plan ahead.

RAISING AWARENESS: WHEN TO DISCLOSE

In the past, I tried to hide my differences and play the part of a neurologi-cally typical teen or young adult. Yet, with hindsight, what I 'saw' as normal was far removed to the neurologically typical version of events. I thought nothing of being upset and throwing a tantrum if a pen was moved a foot away, despite engaging in conversation about a recent football match a few minutes earlier.

I found out the hard way, and it was only when I was unemployed I knew more about 'me' through greater self-awareness. This was in early 2002. Before then, I never thought of myself as having an autism spectrum disorder. I only thought of myself as 'Stuart', who had had several inter-views, though no job at the end, a good memory, and three and a half years' attendance at a special school.

Following an interview with my current employer for an administra-tive position, I was given two assessment tests for a more suitable position. This was the technical vacancy I hold today. This involved cooperation with my local Job Centre, which included an overview of myself.

Prior to then, I had always been wary of ticking the box entitled 'Do You Have A Disability?' or 'Do You Require Any Adjustments To Your Role?' For similar reasons, I had never disclosed that on my curriculum vitae, for fear it might have put off potential employers.

If the box had been ticked, and the outcome in finding the job was suc-cessful, I would only disclose details of your autism spectrum disorder in a pragmatic way. Obviously, this doesn't mean starting work by saying 'Hi, my name is Stuart, and I have Asperger's'. Some of the people who inter-viewed you or perused your application form and (or) curriculum vitae may already know. Some may be unsure about AS. I chose to let them decide for themselves and tell them in a less direct way. For example, if a fellow col-league was in awe of your memory, attention to detail or they wondered about your sensory issues, tell them then. Do this by recommending a few books or websites on the subject. In doing so, show them the most direct and accessible works before the more technical stuff.

When I chose to disclose details of my autism spectrum disorder, I decided only to tell my closest colleagues to avoid possible ridicule or the statement being used against me. Only when others got to know me closer did I choose to tell them. I would recommend being brief and saying something on the lines of: 'I was diagnosed with Asperger Syndrome/ Semantic Pragmatic Language Disorder/high-functioning autism in year X or at Y years of age.' Leave them to ask the questions and accentuate your strengths. You could answer by saying, for example, 'My strengths include good attention to detail', or 'I am independently minded', or 'I'm a determined person', so long as these statements are relevant to your job.

Finally

Having worked for the same employer for over four years, I feel that I have succeeded in raising awareness of autism spectrum disorders to my fellow colleagues. This has resulted in greater rapport with and respect from my immediate colleagues. The writing of this piece is the culmination of having experienced six years in employment and two years of Youth Training. Though adept at catching buses to work and arriving on time, it has only been in the last four years that I have started to master the 'rules' required for holding down a job.

For anyone starting out, new to the labour market, I wish you the best of luck, and don't be afraid of who you are or what you are.

Glossary

Clocking on: The process of starting work by placing a card in a clocking machine which displays the start time. The opposite to this is 'clocking off', which displays the employee's finish time on the card.

Financial year: Unlike the Gregorian calendar which runs from January to December, the UK financial year typically runs from the first day in April to the last day in March of the following year.

Overtime: In this context, extra hours worked beyond the usual hours, either paid or unpaid.

P45: The form handed to you on leaving your previous job, which is retained by your present employer.

P60: The form detailing all tax and National Insurance contributions made in the last financial year. This is retained by the employee.

Signing-on: The term given to describe the fortnightly ritual of proving your availability for work at a local Job Centre.

Youth Training: Founded as the YTS (Youth Training Scheme) in 1983 for 16–18-year-olds in England and Wales, offering a weekly allowance, work skills and day release education at a local college or place of employment. Later known as Youth Training, Careerships and National Traineeships.

Chapter 13: The Importance of Motivation and Clear Communication at Work

Vicky Bliss

Introduction by Luke Beardon

Vicky makes such an important point in this chapter – that of the importance of motivation and understanding exactly why one is expected to do things in a certain way. NTs are generally drawn to jobs that motivate them and that they are good at. It is no different for someone with AS, although the motivation itself may stem from something completely different. This need not matter, so long as the end result is a happy employee and happy employer. Vicky also makes the point that the people with whom one works are as important as the job itself. This is useful advice, and something that should be considered if at all possible. If a group of colleagues or a line manager were open minded and accepting of people, it is likely that a person with AS would be better off than with a more narrow-minded population. The irony being, of course, that we are told it is people with AS who have 'rigidity of thought' – yet rigidity of thought from people who are NT can cause major problems for those with AS!

I was wondering what my qualifications were for writing something about employment and autism. I have, in over 20 years' experience, met about 20 people with autism (all with Asperger Syndrome or High Functioning

Autism) who have been in paid employment. Perhaps double that number have had experiences in voluntary employment. In a context of work over such a long period, I guess I have met about a thousand people who have autism with or without an accompanying learning disability. I am not particularly good at guessing numbers, but I'd say the proportion I've described there is about right.

Additionally, as a psychologist on the autistic side of normal – because my autism is formally undiagnosed and informally identified as eccentricity, oddness, rudeness, stupidity, gullibility, intelligence, thoroughness, straight-forwardness, logic and coldness – I have had...wait a minute, let me count...the following jobs: church organist (voluntary of course; one can't put a price on holiness), waitress (for five days because of my poor social skills, poor short-term memory and very poor overview of the main aims of the job), secretary, befriender (voluntary for two days because of differing views on the appropriateness of 'use of restraint' with the man whom I was befriending – and I was pro-force because he was head-butting me), social worker (twice), director of a learning disability service (a weird turn of events given my poor ability with numbers and the need to manage a $750,000 budget), behaviour consultant, psychologist, senior lecturer at the University of Manchester, senior clinician in psychology, consultant psychologist and head of learning disability service, and now, self-employed solution-focused psychologist. How many is that? Counting the two stints as social worker as two separate jobs (which they were) I think I have had 14 jobs since I was 16 years old. Is that a lot? I have no idea how that compares to the working lives of others.

Does all that qualify me to comment on employment and people with autism? I guess that is for you the reader to decide. What I want to tell you, in case you believe I am qualified, is what I know about the things that help differently abled thinkers, like myself and other people with autism, in the performance of their jobs.

Motivation to work

I am much, much better at jobs when (a) I am interested in the work and (b) I can see the results of my efforts. I can do work in which I am interested even when I can't see the direct effect of my labours. For example, I can read background literature in order to inform my work, even though there is no tangible evidence that the reading will make a difference. I am interested enough to do the work without an obvious outcome. In other circumstances, however, I like to see the outcomes of what I have done and *these outcomes need to be important to me.* I don't care, for example, if a car is clean, so although I can see the results of my efforts, I don't care about those results. I therefore, would not make a good car valet. I am capable of doing absolutely any job I want to do (at least that's what Mom kept saying) but my motivation to do the job is perhaps more critical than my ability to do the job.

Some jobs, like being a waitress, held no interest for me because I did not care whether or not customers were satisfied with the service. They asked for food, I fetched it for them and they gave me money. I put the money in the till, and at the end of the day Loretta gave me money to take home. That was the job from my point of view, but Loretta, the café owner (and my godmother, bless her, which prevented her from inflicting actual bodily harm) wanted a waitress who didn't see things in such a black-and-white way. Though of course neither of us knew that when she hired me.

I used to say 'What can I get ya?' and write what they said very neatly on a little pad. I would go get their drinks first, because Loretta had told me to do that and it made sense to me. She also wanted me to tell her what food they had asked for, but I didn't know this at first so I never told her. I figured it was a small café, I knew she was listening and could hear what they said, so I thought she would set about her job of cooking whilst I did my job of getting drinks. She said, 'Aren't you going to tell me what they want?' and I said, 'Couldn't you hear them?' and she simply said, 'Just give me the paper once you've written down what they need. And write a bit faster if you can.' Well done her. Good, clear communication of expectations without extra words about social skills. We got on very well at that point. I had been on the job for an hour.

Then she used to say 'Order's up!' when she had put their food on a plate. Much like a smart pet who knows what to do when someone says 'sit', I knew this meant that something someone had ordered was ready to take to the table, though I could never quite get what 'Order's up!' meant. 'Up where? Up what? Had it been down?' I used to take the food and put it on any available space at the table. I didn't speak to the punters because everything was self-evident, and I didn't think to remember who ordered what because they were the ones who wanted it so I figured they could remember what they ordered or just grab the food nearest them, I had no preference on the matter. I would plonk the plates down and walk away to stand behind the counter and await my next victims.

As the week wore on, Loretta used to say 'Saints preserve us' and shake her head at me. I thought that odd because she didn't look the religious type but if praying was what she wanted to do it made no difference to me. It turns out that she thought I would remember who ordered what, and I swear to you, that never entered my mind. She thought that I would remember it by writing it down though that was absurd logic unless I also wrote the names of people beside what they'd ordered. Writing a list of food doesn't help me remember to whom the food belongs! I used to say 'Jeepers' (because I wasn't as religious as Loretta with her invocation to the saints) and shake my head at her. We each thought the other to be quite addled.

But Dad said she was the boss, so I tried to do what she said. Hot roast beef goes to fat man with feed cap and red jacket; hamburger and fries to kid with snotty nose; chef salad to woman in green coat who just divorced her husband I happen to know, and chicken sandwich to that lonely person by the door who owes my dad money. I can already spot the problems with this; man removes cap and objects to being called fat, kid wipes nose, woman takes green coat off and people move tables...that sort of thing. Plus I had to remember their drinks too. And there were café noises and distracting activity and my short-term memory kept sparking out, even though my short-term memory for some things was exceptional, as Loretta often noted. But poor Loretta's face just kept getting redder and redder when I would tell people to move back to their original seat rather than switch their meals around. Or when I would say too loudly that the hot roast beef dinner belonged to the fat man next to the snotty nosed kid. Or when I remembered too much detail about the private life of who ordered the honey roast ham. Honestly, I worried for the woman's blood pressure. It transpired that although it appeared I had all the individual skills to do the waitressing job, I was not sufficiently motivated by any aspect of the work to find it interesting. Even though I could see the outcomes of my work, I simply didn't care if people were happy with the service. It never occurred to me to be interested in this.

What helps?

CONTEXT

I, and others like me, frequently seem to lack the 'big picture' of the jobs we are asked to do. In the absence of a clearly described context for the work, we are left to make up our own ideas about why we are doing what we are doing. In the example above, I simply did not know that the café had several aims. The main aim is to do whatever is necessary, within the law, to bring punters in and encourage them to spend their money. What I had established as the main aim of the café was really only one way of meeting a bigger aim. Other aims of the café were to provide a pleasant, social atmosphere in which food could be enjoyed, to provide good food for not too much money, to provide a comfortable place where people could meet and talk to other people, to provide a bulletin board of community events, to provide a bit of escapism for the humdrum of daily life. Jeepers. I thought they only wanted food! Had I been hired to make people want to come in and spend money, I would have been mentally prepared for a wider range of activities than just plonking food down in front of customers. I still may have messed up the job, but Loretta's blood pressure wouldn't have suffered nearly so much.

Sadly, employers often think that the overall context in which their employees work is implicitly understood, and if pushed to describe an overall aim along with how an individual's job fits into that aim, they find they are unable to do this. This makes me think that this kind of exercise would be beneficial to more employees and employers than just those with autism. If employers have to clearly describe the context of their work, they have to be clear about details that perhaps they have never had to describe before. For example, people assume that cleaning staff in hospitals are important to the overall aim of the hospital, but few people can state the details of why they are important and who would notice if they were not doing a good job.

CLEAR EXPECTATIONS

It is, I think, impossible to spend too much time on setting out clear expectations for an employee. Neurotypical people tend to assume everyone is using language in the same way they are, which is not so, certainly of people with autism but I suspect even with other neurotypical people. Many people with autism are happy to do what is asked of them, as long as it makes sense to them (which is part of setting it in the wider context of the business) and provided they understand in practical terms what the boss wants. For example, Loretta wanted customers to feel happy about coming into her café, and one way she would know they were happy to come in was if they made a positive comment about her waitresses or about the service. I thought they came in because they were hungry and we were the only café in town. Happy customers never entered into my view of my job. If Loretta had said that one of the markers she would be looking for was positive comments from punters, I would have had a different mindset for my work. I suppose she assumed I knew this, but early on in our working relationship it became apparent that I didn't know this. Employees behaving in ways that don't fit with the overall aim of the business may simply mean they are unclear about the overall aim.

CLEAR PERFORMANCE APPRAISAL

Following on from clear expectations is clear feedback on performance of the job. Many businesses pride themselves on being 'investors in their workforce' and part of this status requires the employers to have a system of performance monitoring and feedback. In the NHS this is meant to happen at least once a year, where boss and bossed get together to review aims and objectives, goals met and training needs etc., for both the past and the coming year. This is exactly the right idea, and for people with autism it is especially good as long as the performance indicators are clear. It has been my experience that performance appraisals contain quite a lot of items such as 'Dresses appropriately for the job' or 'Works well in a team'. These items may be fine for neurotypical people but mean little to a literal, logically minded person. An employer will need to go into a bit more detail in order to make these criteria useful.

'Works well in a team', for example: by whose standards is this judged? An employer needs to know how they will decide if I work well in a team, and tell me how this will be decided before my behaviour is judged against this standard. Will the employer ask other team members if I work well with them? Will it depend upon what the team produces? Will it depend upon how often I am seen working with team members? Will it depend on how often I socialize with team members? Will I need to be 'liked' by the team or will being effective within the team be enough? Does the employer want me to make team members laugh? What is the accepted way for me to disagree with a team member? What things might happen within the team that the boss would want me to tell them right away?

There are a million questions that come to my mind when working well as a team member is one of the employment criteria.

Employers can't, of course, be expected to have the answers to each and every possible question about each and every performance criterion. More's the pity because life would be a lot simpler for me if they could! What has helped me in this regard is employers being open to my seemingly endless questions and worries about this kind of vague criterion. I need to be able to ask my boss, 'How will you know if I am working well as a team?' Bosses don't often like this question because their answer is 'I don't know how I will know...I will just know', but of course they can't say that, so they feel pressure to come up with some good way that they will know. I need a boss who will take the time to work out with me how they will know if I am meeting the criteria. Even if we can only come up with tentative ideas about how 'working well with a team' will be judged, that is a good start. What I will want to do then is keep giving the boss feedback on how our tentative criteria is working so that we can change them or further define them as we learn more about how a 'good team member' is actually defined. I wish employers would trust me that efforts in this area will benefit the entire workforce, not just people with autism. In fact, people with autism, with their mind for detail, are exactly the right people to have in a job to help employers figure out how good performance can be measured!

COMFORT WITH DIFFERENTLY ABLED PEOPLE
Bosses who are willing to bend and to learn more about themselves, about their job and about their workers are just the right kind of bosses for me. I cannot get along with a boss who believes they know everything, though I can respect a boss who knows more than me in some areas, if they acknowledge I know more than them in other areas. In this respect, I am not unreasonable! Sometimes a work situation requires immediate action from the boss, and I accept that they may need to say 'Don't do that again', without asking for any more information. I need to be clear about what they mean by 'that', however, so I do need to be able to revisit this after the boss's breathing and blood pressure have stabilized. This is not because I am being awkward, but because I am being me, and a good employee, by making sure I understand the detail of whatever I did that was wrong.

Equally, there are other situations when a boss can afford to take a bit more time with the employee and rather than saying, 'Don't do that again', they can take the softer, more intelligent approach of 'Help me understand why you did that'. In explaining my behaviour to the boss I get to understand myself better, I feel the boss is interested in my different views, and I become much more open to negotiation regarding my future behaviour. I would estimate that 80 per cent of the time, when I have this discussion with someone who is supervising my work I end up saying, 'Really?! I never knew that!' because the supervisor is applying some principle of human behaviour that I never thought about before. This is extremely helpful because I can gauge my future behaviour in a new light.

I often wondered in the course of my working life, why work colleagues did not like me. Quite a few work colleagues did like me, and I am ever so glad of that, but a significant number appeared not to like me and I had such a high opinion of my logical self that I could not understand why they wouldn't like me. I knew (and this is still true) that from the time I woke up to the time I went to sleep I was always trying hard to do the right thing. I would chronically scan my environment and ask questions, either to help myself understand someone else's behaviour or to understand what other people expected of me. 'Do you want me to do this or that?' 'Shall I do that now or later?' 'Does one eat this with a fork or spoon?' I would look intensely at everything and everyone simply to gain clues about what was going on, and what my role was meant to be. People used to tell me I was highly strung, to which I would say 'Is that good or bad?' and they would do the Loretta shake of the head (though as I got older the 'Saints preserve us' was replaced by things more akin to 'Piss off'). I cannot help being like this because I don't know how to 'just be'. If I don't analyse, intellectualize or think my way through a day, I simply fall asleep. A boss who can tolerate this apparently endless analysing and wondering and seeking of answers is the boss for me. I need one who takes my questions at face value, and who responds with the same respect for fact and logic if possible.

BENEFIT OF THE DOUBT – EMPLOYER WHO ASKS FOR HELP UNDERSTANDING
An employer who is at ease with someone who is differently abled will, I guess, be pretty self-assured and will not take the chronic autistic questions as a personal insult. When I am analysing behaviour, wondering what my role is, wondering how people will know if I am a good employee etc., I need a boss who doesn't assume I am being an ass, trying to get people into

trouble, trying to be 'top dog' or trying to make other people feel inferior. Apparently people with autism are targets for these kind of assumptions when, usually, the person is trying hard to make sense of a situation. A self-assured boss who understands about differently abled people is one who will ask questions of me in order to gain more information or insight into my behaviour.

I have been told that some bosses do not like to ask their workers for clarification because they worry about appearing dumb. I don't want them to appear dumb, but I worry quite a lot that if they don't ask for information about why I do the things I do, they may feel smarter but will think that I am being an ass. I almost never want to be an ass, I hate being 'top dog' (too much responsibility being on top) and I would never, ever try to make someone else feel inferior (unless I was in a frisky mood and they were trying to convince me they were superior…then I might). If I ask whether I ought to eat something with a fork or spoon, it is because I want to do the right thing, and do not know whether or not I ought to use a fork or spoon, not because I am trying to make a disparaging remark about the food, as has happened before. If I behave in a way that someone else thinks is unprofessional, it is very likely that I will be able to explain exactly why I did what I did (because everything I do has been examined) without taking offence. I need that self-assured boss who is going to ask me why I did this thing that someone else has complained about, and then who is going to listen to my reasons. The boss need not agree with my behaviour or my reasons, but they do need to listen and talk through how they would like me to handle future situations.

If I am standing still whilst others are in a flurry of activity, I need a boss who doesn't assume I am stupid or bone idle. I need someone to tell me, amongst all the activity, what it is that I ought to be doing. It is the honest truth that when I am in the middle of high emotion and buzzing activity without knowing my role, I will stand frozen and try to disappear. The same is true if I am surrounded by people who are only telling me what NOT to do. In the presence of criticism without discussion, I will freeze so as not to do anything to attract more criticism. I hate what I call blind, senseless criticism that is more about making the person who is saying it feel good and nothing at all about giving me instructions as to what I ought to be doing instead. I need the boss who can tell me if I am doing something wrong, listen to why I did it, then instruct me in a different way to behave in future situations. And I need a boss who can repeat this procedure over and over and over as different situations arise. For this boss, I will give my life in loyalty.

FREQUENT REINFORCEMENT OF GOOD STUFF

And finally, I need the boss who will frequently find things that I am doing right and tell me about them. This can be done in a 'hit and run' kind of way where they might say 'I liked the way you did that report' or something similar. I especially work well for those bosses who notice and name my particular strengths and skills, and can make reference to those when they are asking me to do something. For example, 'Because you are so good at artwork, I would like you to design a cover for our annual report'. It is true I will besiege them with questions about the detail of the report cover, but it will be the product of my very best efforts if I think they are relying on my particular talents.

And people with autism have a lot of talents. Bags of them. We different-thinkers are worth the effort if you want a good employee. Time off sick is usually rare. Adherence to schedules is usually exceptional. Following clear instructions is usually done reliably. Problem-solving, trouble-shooting and even working with customers can be a forte given the right support. As my mom used to say, and I believe she was speaking for everyone like me, we can do whatever we want to do. It's the wanting to that makes the difference.

Chapter 14: Continuing to Search for the Right Job for Me

Philip Bricher

Introduction by Luke Beardon

Philip notes how his experiences of the Job Centre were less than helpful. It strikes me that employment services, including Connexions, could be the difference between successful employment and either unsuccessful employment or unemployment for many people with AS. However, such organizations themselves are not well supported to gain the appropriate training that may enable them to understand better the population of people with AS, and thus in turn support them in a better way. The potential impact of statutory training in AS for employment services is huge, and yet at present it does not exist.

I remember the times towards age 16 when I would see the careers advisor at school, to predicate future plans. I could not imagine a time when I would cease the daily pattern I had known for so many years. Regarding future plans, my take was that 'I dream too much and yet I worry too much'. I used to expect I would make my livelihood from performing and composing, the latter which I was more passionate about doing then, despite having learnt so much since! In any case, the question was put on hold, as I stayed in education for rather longer, through sixth form and then university.

The only time I have worked near to full-time was the summer prior to my commencement at university, where I was delivering leaflets for a supermarket. Primarily, my only success in finding work has been in the 'distribution industry', delivering newspapers, take-away menus, election leaflets, you name it. However, more recently, I have been able to earn more money by playing at weddings, funerals and 'run-of-the-mill' Sunday services. (And I used to sing at weddings as a chorister.)

On leaving university (a year late due to needing an extra year to catch up with the workload), I had dreamt that life would be beds of roses, and had hoped that my support worker would help me to land in a field of successful work. However, given that at the same time, I was also moving into independent accommodation that sucked out more than 100 per cent of our allotted hours! After that, we had our disagreements as to how to effect this process, then she went on long-term sick leave, with no talk of a replacement for almost three months (the far side of my birthday). Unfortunately, the iron was not struck whilst hot, and things were left by the wayside, such that the dust and the rust set in. As when I was in a similar position with (lack of) support at university, I felt quite disoriented, succumbed to depression and had no idea where to turn or where I was going. Many people would instinctively say that for advice accessing employment, as well as impact on benefits, I should make enquiries with the Job Centre. However, that has proved less than useful, as they have expected me to reel off definitive plans to them, without attempting to formulate my humble efforts to think of ideas into any concrete plans! Had they done so, I might have had more encouragement at the earlier stages with seeking employment. (Since then I have heard from people on autism support mailing lists of similar experiences, and that staff at such places are oft 'ex-unemployed'.)

At the present day, after a little hassle following enquiries with the local volunteer centre, I am doing a couple of afternoons' admin work, generally data input at a local charity office. The work is rather monotonous, although I appreciate dealing in terms of postcodes, telephone codes and district councils, in which I specialize. Also, a new worker joined the office (a friend of his predecessor) who is interesting to talk to, being quite knowledgeable. This has done wonders to brighten up an otherwise dull time. Further encouragement falls in respect of Christian teachings (in which I am instilled) of servanthood, rather than, power, prosperity etc. In this sense, doing less reputed/interesting/lucrative work, putting the benefit of others before mine own. However, I wonder that it is the best way to utilize my God-given potential! This is where it is hard to differentiate between autism and spiritual matters!!

However, I have yet other routes down which to follow enquiries. Many people I meet at conventions etc., come up with constructive ideas (sadly more so than recent/current support workers), which could essentially spread me thin, and may display little awareness to niches based on their ideas. I cannot tell whether it is an Aspie thing or not that I struggle to identify how my skills and interests are best put to use, possibly not from various conversations I have been privy to. However I do gather that many environments would not suit me, where I may get overloaded, exhausted or struggle to meet the social climate of that workplace. As it is, at the time of writing, I have had two bad nights of sleep this week, easily attributed to over-stimulation. This is where I seem to lack the discernment of how much I can physically manage, as if I am suffering this level of bad effects with my relatively limited work schedule, how much worse would it be if I were pressured to get up early repeatedly and curbed what personal chores I could expect to accomplish in the daytime?

Chapter 15: I'm Just So Willing to Work

Emma Beard

Introduction by Luke Beardon

Emma sums it all up in her title – so willing to work. Many people with AS are
perate to work, yet still find themselves either in jobs that are unsuitable or ind
priate, or not in work at all. The loss to society is huge; financially, obvion
more importantly the impact it has on the individuals themselves, who oft
depressed and unmotivated. Emma's mum is also very perceptive in whd
and sums it up very well. It is clearly not easy having AS in the workpl
be easy being a parent. Supporting the whole family is an import
process, and yet one which gets neglected far too often.

When I left college I went to a training service in Che
me as a classroom helper in a county primary schoc
area. I was placed in a reception class. The teacher
the placement. I was called 'Miss' and I found it v
responsible job and I found both the noise and
Although I didn't show it, I reacted inwardly
wardly by shouting at a child. The job in
setting of a responsible job role which w

The next job placement I had was in
work was fine as long as I was doing se

without an expectation that I had to take the initiative. In this setting bullying could occur as well as unstructured social interaction which I found tough. I was happier just getting on with set tasks quietly and focusing on those.

When I left college I was placed in the available jobs rather than those which capitalized on my strengths. There was no guidance available about how to look at the strengths my AS brings, and also the weaknesses. Luckily, however, purely by chance someone made a remark that I might be good with computers. I have found my niche in computers where the environment is quiet. My key strengths centre around data input and typing. These tasks capitalize on my strengths of focus, attention to detail, accuracy and a high work output doing set tasks with clear instructions.

In retrospect on leaving college I should have been assessed properly instead of being sent to the available jobs which were inevitably inappropriate for my abilities. Not having this happen has impacted on my confidence and has been a bad experience. My skills should have been identified earlier and acted upon. What disappoints me is the lack of funding for specialist AS employment schemes. I would like employers to see more positive AS role models rather than the stereotypes such as Roy Cropper in the soap *Coronation Street*. I would like to see these role models dressed smartly doing well in mainstream jobs where they are not just tolerated but respected and appreciated. I would like to see employers recognizing more of the good points that AS brings as well as tolerating the problems the condition brings.

To support me at work I need colleagues to take account of my needs associated with AS which they find hard to do sometimes as I come across as articulate and intelligent, having an invisible condition. The best thing they can do is let me get on with tasks without the interruption of chatting and social interaction and the associated noise of multiple conversations. Talking more slowly and providing written instructions really helps. Also, people to be straightforward and as blunt as possible, saying what they mean and expect is essential: get to the point and don't waffle. Supporting the sensory environment really helps too. For example, noise disturbs me greatly, I need people to be patient and quiet so that I can focus and concentrate. Not having this support, for example, was a nightmare on the till in the charity shop. Expecting me to do more than one thing at once is a struggle too.

I am lucky that I did have one great placement working in a council office setting. This worked out well as the people were supportive, kind and understanding which goes a really long way. I managed to get this placement through someone my mum knew. My ideal job involves typing and data input and only those tasks. Simple as it may sound to have such a job out there, it is surprising how many employers expect multi-tasking and such roles have been sporadic.

Anne Beard – Emma's mum

The main issue with Emma has always been that she has been misjudged. Employers have not realized how Emma's AS affects her and how much she can retain and cope with. I have been guilty of this too with Emma since she is so intelligent and comes across so well. I have under-estimated how much Emma can struggle. I have assumed that Emma's AS would recede as she gets older. This has happened. However, she has been tested, constantly reminded of her deficiencies and judged over the last 12 years, while in the wrong environment. I feel that this has taken its toll. She is uneasy and fears not remembering when in a new situation. This also happens at home when being shown new household skills or cooking. Any new employer needs to understand how Emma learns and to keep things as ordered and systematic as possible. Emma has a big skill and qualification in her computing but only that skill. She needs a job narrowly using that skill only. She doesn't thrive on having too many new additions to a job routine and doesn't thrive on having too much responsibility thrown at her.

Emma is an excellent employee. She is extremely loyal and motivated and in the right environment is a real asset. Another quality Emma has is her ability to be tenacious and never give up despite her many setbacks. She shows great stoicism and character. These traits are a bonus for any employer.

List of Contributors

Emma Beard is single and, she says, likely to remain so! She has taken several night-school classes in word processing in order to gain a marketable skill, and has recently started a job with her local authority. She is hopeful that this will be successful as it is repetitive typing in an AS-friendly environment and she isn't required to multi-task. She has typical AS, but can be quite sociable if she's in the mood.

John Biddulph has worked in education organizations in a variety of roles for the past thirty years. He holds first degrees in music and art history, a Master's degree researching creativity using microtechnology and special educational needs, and a PhD from Trinity College, Cambridge researching online virtual learning environments. He is a qualified teacher, published and recorded composer, ECB level 2 cricket coach and a terrible dancer. John is married with three children and a pet cat. The cat does not have Asperger Syndrome but John does. Along with his wife Fiona, John regularly provides inputs to conferences and courses on autism.

Paul Binks has been a manager in a local authority for five years, working in the field of performance management. He gained his MBA in 2002 and is a member of the Chartered Management Institute. Paul manages the small team in which Dean Worton works.

E. Veronica (Vicky) Bliss recognizes many, many indicators of AS in her own personal history, but the condition for her is as yet undiagnosed. She has worked for over 20 years with people who have autism as well as people with other differences and has worked as a solution-focused psychologist for the past six years.

Philip Bricher was taken out of mainstream school when it was obvious that something about him was different (and difficult?). He was placed in a Designated Special Provision of a mainstream school for a time, and there he first heard of autism. It was not until upper school that he heard of AS, and throughout university he learnt much more about it. With concessions, he completed his degree (at the University of Northampton) in Music and French with a 2:1 (Hons). Philip can be contacted via Jessica Kingsley Publishers.

Alexandra Brown prefers to be known as Alex. She lives with her partner and teenaged daughter in North Yorkshire. She has worked full-time for the past seven years within library services. She loves books but isn't always so fond of the people! Alex received her diagnosis of AS in 2007 at the age of 38. She enjoys writing, mainly for her friends, and uses writing to analyse her thoughts and make sense of the world around her.

Cornish was diagnosed with AS in 2003 at the age of 44. Since then he has become a qualified expert in AS. Cornish is an executive board member of his local autism charity, and has worked for the past five years with adolescents and adults with ASDs. He runs an informal telephone helpline and is part of an adult AS support group. Cornish is an experienced trainer, and speaks comprehensively on his own personal perspective of living with the challenges and joys of AS. Anyone wishing to contact Cornish can do so through the publishers (please do).

Mark Haggarty was diagnosed with AS at the age of 26. Despite never knowing what sort of work he wanted to do, he has not experienced any difficulty holding down jobs and currently works in accountancy. He has cycled London to Paris twice, raising money for charities (including the National Autistic Society, UK) and plans to undertake a longer cycle from London to Geneva. Mark is a Francophile, interested in all aspects of France, French language and culture, and is also into grabatology (if you don't know what that is, a good dictionary or the internet will reveal all!).

Giles Harvey was diagnosed with Asperger Syndrome in 1997 at the age of 22. He has had several jobs including working for a large charity in North West England that supports people with a diagnosis of AS. It was from this post that Giles developed a further interest in and knowledge of AS.

Anne Henderson's son had been labelled with every possible label and was eventually diagnosed with AS at age 27: he was sectioned under the Mental Health Act in 2004. After two years on a forensic ward receiving the right care he has moved into residential accommodation and has just started his second year at mainstream college. For the first time in his life he, his sister and mother are able to lead happier lives as he has appropriate support to achieve his independence and ambitions.

PJ Hughes is a civil servant. He was diagnosed with AS in 1999. He gives talks about his experiences and often writes articles as well. He is the author of *Reflections: Me and Planet Weirdo*, published by Chipmunka Publishing.

Steve Jarvis lives alone in Hertfordshire and has lived on his own all his adult life. He works as a learning consultant and has been in full-time employment all his life, but has never had any success with relationships. He was diagnosed with Asperger Syndrome when he was 45 years old.

Chris Mitchell was diagnosed with AS at university, aged 20. Since his diagnosis, Chris has completed his MA (Hons) in information and library management at the University of Northumbria, where he completed a dissertation on the impact of autism emailing lists. Currently, he works as a clerical assistant for an educational psychology service, and in his spare time is an advocate for AS, giving talks and workshops on the subject as well as providing training for potential employers and frontline services. His autobiography, *Glass Half-Empty, Glass Half-Full*, is published by Sage Publishing.

Neil Shepherd was diagnosed with AS when he was 31 after struggling for years to hold down a job in the IT industry, remain sane and do all of the things that 'normal' people do. Married, divorced and now happily living with his Aspergic girlfriend Emily, he is still struggling to hold down a job in the IT industry. He has also written a book about his experiences, *Wired Up Wrong*, published by lulu.com publishing.

Stuart Vallantine is a poet and visual artist on the autism spectrum, diagnosed with Semantic Pragmatic Language Disorder at the age of seven. In his early years, he was regarded as 'autistic' and 'hyperactive'. In recent years, he has recited examples of his work and spoken at lectures relating to AS and similar autism spectrum disorders.

Dean Worton has a positive expression of AS and lives in north west England. He has worked as a performance data administrator in the public sector for two years and has previously worked in a number of administration roles in the private and voluntary sectors. He is supported by an employment scheme for people with disabilities and in his spare time runs an internet social and support group for adults with AS who live in the UK.

Index